MOSQUITO

Some of the design and development team of the Mosquito in May 1943 with the fighter prototype W4052 behind. Under the technical leadership of Capt de Havilland and C. C. Walker, they are from left to right: R. E. Bishop, chief designer; F. W. Plumb, experimental shop superintendent; W. A. Tamblin, senior designer; P. F. Bryan, chief draughtsman; R. M. Clarkson, assistant chief engineer, head of aerodynamics; D. King; J. K. Crowe; G. W. Drury; C. T. Wilkins, assistant chief designer; R. Hutchinson; C. F. Willis; Rex King; R. H. Harper, chief structural engineer; D. R. Newman; F. T. Watts; R. M. Hare; M. Herrod-Hempswell; F. J. Hamilton; J. P. Smith; E. H. King; R. J. Nixon; A. G. Peters; G. C. I. Gardiner. (BAE Systems)

MOSQUITO

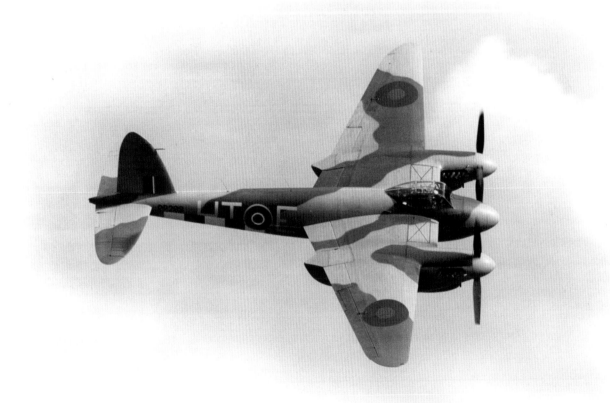

Mark Nelson

MIDLAND

An imprint of
Ian Allan Publishing

Introduction and Acknowledgements

THE Second World War was to see a rapid escalation in the design of ever more sophisticated weaponry in the arsenals of the world's leading powers and no more so than in the development of aircraft. Into this arena entered the De Havilland Mosquito in November 1940 which, for some, was a throwback to another age due to its all-wooden construction and initially unarmed configuration. Doubting contractors were soon eating humble pie as this remarkable aircraft proved to be extremely fast, manoeuvrable and highly adaptable to a multitude of tasks, all of which it undertook with great success: bomber, fighter, fighter-bomber, night-fighter, photo and weather reconnaissance, pathfinder, civil mail carrier, trainer, torpedo-fighter/bomber, torpedo-reconnaissance fighter/fighter-bomber, target tug, civil aerial survey and more. It was a winner from the start. Few other aircraft of that period were so adaptable, except perhaps Germany's Junkers Ju 88 to some degree. In modern parlance, the Mosquito was a true multi-role aircraft.

Many books and magazine articles have been written over the years on the Mosquito and I cannot hope to encapsulate all that the aircraft and, more importantly, its crews did with this aircraft within these modest pages. My hope is to give the reader a taste of the Mosquito from construction to operations in some of its more famous and perhaps the not so famous roles, backed up by some fascinating and rarely seen photographs and related material.

This book could not have happened without the support and assistance of many. Foremost is Robert Forsyth of Chevron Publishing who encouraged me to 'pick up the pen' and has been of great assistance in the genesis of the book. Others whom I'd like to thank are: Ken Merrick, Barry Spicer, David Wadman, Sally Forsyth, Eddie Creek, Derek Bedwell (ex Rolls-Royce), Simon Watson, Roly Fane, Bob Cowper (ex 456 Sqdn), David Smith (ex 692 Sqdn), Glyn Powell: Mosquito Aircraft Restorations NZ, Dr Andy Dawson, Robert Fox, Chris Goss, John Howell (ex 418 Sqdn), Stephen Skinner, David Coeshall, Bob Glasby, William 'Bill' Zuk, Melanie Robson: Flight International, Stephen Lewis, Michael Davies, Trevor Friend: BAE Systems, Peter Verney (ex 39 Sqdn), Richard de Boer and associates of the Calgary Mosquito Society, Warren Denholm: Avspecs NZ, Ravery Guillaume, Allan MacNutt, Les Homer, Mark Postlethwaite: WW2 Images, Peter Cromer, Kimberly Ingram: Victoria Air Maintenance Ltd, Janusz Swiatlon, Scott & Trevor McTavish, Brian Doherty, Philip Nelson, Bomber Command Museum of Canada, Trevor Dean and staff at the Australian Aviation Museum. A special thanks to David Vincent, Bruce Graham and Jackie.

Back on Sunday 4 November 1990 I was privileged to be at Salisbury Hall to witness a celebration of the 50th Anniversary of the first flight of the prototype Mosquito, with probably the largest gathering of ex-flight and ground crews to be seen together in quite some time. When Mosquito T. III, RR299 arrived later in the day and commenced a superb display over the museum, I tore my gaze away from her and looked along the silent ranks of elderly men who, with upturned faces, watched her with great interest and affection and, no doubt, many a triggered memory. Dare I say, I detected a trembling lip and a moist eye in many of them.

To Mum and Dad: I wish you both could have seen this book.

First published 2012

ISBN 978 85780 334 1

© Mark Nelson 2012
Project Editor and Production: Chevron Publishing Limited
Cover and book design: Mark Nelson
© Colour profiles: Janusz Swiatlon

Published by Midland Publishing
An imprint of Ian Allan Publishing Ltd, Riverside Business Park, Molesey Road, Hersham, Surrey, KT12 4RG
Printed by Ian Allan Printing Ltd, Riverside Business Park, Molesey Road, Hersham, Surrey, KT12 4RG
Code: 1207/x

Visit the Ian Allan Publishing website at **www.ianallanpublishing.com**

CONTENTS

To fly a very, very long way...

Boost high, revs low,
You'll be surprised how far you go.
Fly at rated height and trim it,
Stretch your journey to the limit.

PUBLISHED BY DE HAVILLAND AIRCRAFT
OF CANADA LTD. TORONTO 1944

FOREWORD

Squadron Leader Bob Cowper (Rtd)
DFC & Bar, OAM, National Order of the Legion of Honour (Fr)

A recent photograph of Bob Cowper in Adelaide, South Australia.

I T was my privilege to pilot the de Havilland Mosquito as a night-fighter during my service with 456 RAAF Night Fighter Squadron in the UK in WW2. I was a Flight Commander and Acting CO at the war's end and I have much love and respect for this aircraft.

So much has been written about this versatile aircraft, firstly in its role as Photo Reconnaissance when it was the fastest operational aircraft in the skies at the time, then to its ground strafing suitability destroying trains and many other ground targets. Next to the Night Fighter variant and then to the incredible bomber version carrying a 4000 lb bomb as far as Berlin. What a wonder of an aircraft and so damn good looking and a joy to look at.

My deep respect came from the sheer pleasure that it was to fly. In spite of some reports of swinging on take-off, which

I think were unfounded, the Mosquito had no nasty flying traits and I would be dead now if it wasn't so sturdy under some shocking weather conditions we encountered at times. In my case being caught in a storm with so much ice, hail and lightning that we were lucky to survive. My regard for the aircraft only increased.

The ability of the Mosquito to fly on one engine is legendary, as hundreds of pilots who have flown and landed on one engine will testify, and it certainly gave the crew a feeling of security.

A fine pencil portrait by Barry Spicer of Bob Cowper, showing him about a month after he joined 456 Squadron at the commencement of his second tour of operations – see page 88. His first tour included operations with 89 and 108 Squadrons in Malta. Top left: Also by the same artist, Mosquito NF. XVII, RX-D, HK356 frequently flown by Cowper and his navigator/radar operator Bill Watson. (Courtesy © Barry Spicer, www.barryspicer.com)

Members of 456 Squadron including Bob Cowper ninth from left, front row, with a Mosquito T. III at RAF Ford. Bill Watson, Cowper's navigator is seated far right. Seated sixth from right is Col Griffin, also from Adelaide, who at time of press still flies around 50 hours a year in his RV-6 – see page 79.

This beautiful aircraft was ideal for Night Fighting because of its sheer response and speed when pursuing the target. Many of our trips involved night intruding well into enemy territory covering enemy airfields in support of our bombers on their raids. We were often in the air for five or more hours. We had moderate success destroying Buzz Bombs and although our aircraft were cluttered with airborne radar our Squadron succeeded in destroying 29 of them.

It was this beautiful aircraft which enabled myself and our Squadron to make a modest but worthwhile contribution to winning the air war in WW2 by destroying 42 enemy aircraft.

14 February 1945

Day Ranger - Denmark

CONFIDENTIAL

FL Tony ____
FO Roy LeLong
FO 'Mac' McLaren
FO John Waters

Left: Two Mosquito FB. VIs of the RAF's Fighter Experimental Flight (FEF) in their revetments at the north-east corner of Ford airfield in Sussex, England in late 1944. Armed with four nose-mounted .303 inch Browning machine guns and four under-belly 20 mm cannon, it was the Mosquitoes from this unit which were detailed to attack 6./KG 200's base at Tirstrup in February 1945. TA386 was an FB. VI Series ii, powered by Merlin 25s and was one of a batch of 20 built at Hatfield in early 1945. Series ii's had a number of detail differences to the Series i, were distinguishable by the absence of the radio mast behind the cockpit and a bulged side canopy blister for the navigator.

DATE, 14 February 1945: two Mosquito FB. VIs of the Fighter Experimental Flight (FEF) at Ford, in Sussex, were detailed for an operation against a little known *Luftwaffe* airfield at Tirstrup on the east coast of Denmark. This Mosquito unit was formed on 27 October 1944 out of the Central Fighter Establishment based at Tangmere using a nucleus of very experienced crews equipped with Mosquito FB.VI fighter-bombers. Its role was to conduct 'Intruder' or 'Day Ranger' operations over the Baltic coast and southern Germany. Sorties were usually to an assigned target and on the return flight targets of opportunity were to be sought.

After weather had thwarted two previous attempts to reach Tirstrup that month, a third mission was planned for 14 February. A member of the unit who was to fly on the operation that day was F/O John Waters, who joined the Flight as a navigator in late 1944. He recalls: 'All members of the Fighter Experimental Flight were experienced and had completed at least one tour of operations – except me; I was the only 'sprog' member. So I was very lucky to have an experienced pilot from the start. These pilots were all previous members of 418 Squadron or 605 Squadron, plus two pilots from 23 Squadron. I had always assumed that when 418 and 605 Squadrons were posted to 2nd TAF after D-Day, 11 Group was determined to maintain an Intruder element of a few experienced crews. The full strength was nominally six crews (which we hardly ever were!), with replacements "as applicable".'

The two Mosquitoes were crewed by Roy LeLong, a New Zealander, with F/O J.A. 'Mac' McLaren as his navigator and Tony Craft, with John Waters as his navigator. At 0840 hours the

Flying Officer John Waters of the Fighter Experimental Flight flew as navigator on one of the Mosquitoes which attacked Tirstrup on 14 February 1945: 'I can still see those "pick-a-back" aircraft – and our frustration when the bloody guns got stuck. I can also see the ground crews scattering, such was our surprise visit!'

Mosquitoes were airborne from Ford heading towards Manston, before setting course over the North Sea at 'zero feet', thankfully this time in clear weather. Low and fast, the two Mosquitoes raced across the sea making landfall at Stadil, north of Ringkobing on the east coast of Jutland then turning south for Tuno, where the course was altered for the target. The time was 1056 hours.

John Waters remembers: 'Mac's job was chief navigator; mine was second navigator, just to keep a check, but mainly to make sure we were not "jumped". We had 50 gallon drop tanks, the fuel from which was siphoned into the wing tanks just before reaching the Danish coast. The pilot then pressed the "tit" and the tanks dropped off. But there was no such luck for us on this occasion – press as much as Tony Craft could, they refused to drop off and remained firmly secured to the wings throughout the trip! R/T silence was the order of the day until one reached the target. But on reaching Mariager, Roy LeLong phoned up beseeching my pilot that it would be better for the Deity's sake to drop the bloody drop tanks. It was a fascinating but short conversation!'

John Waters continues: 'This was a hard winter – ice and snow and floods all added to the excitement of map reading and, in my humble opinion, Mac did a good job in finding the airfield so quickly. At least we found it before they found us, and that was very important!'

Just before 1110 hours, the two Mosquitoes approached Tirstrup and commenced their first attack run. John Waters continues: 'On what I assume was a well-defended airfield such as this, we didn't want to hang around; this attack would have lasted no longer than 1 to 2 minutes. The whole essence was surprise – hence the low level – and as soon as the Hun gunners got going, we would have cleared off very smartly. I suppose it was like large calibre clay pigeon shooting as far as they were concerned, and they were pretty good at it too! Once the Flak started, the *strict rule* was to *beat it*! There was, very much from the pilot's point of view, an art in strafing; if you came in too low, then you flew through the stuff that the cannon threw up. The four 20 mm cannon were not parallel to the fore and aft axis of the aircraft – the muzzles were inclined downwards, hence one needed a bit of height for strafing. But if you were too high, your navigator got the twitch because he could see where the Flak was coming from – neither very healthy! Since we were following Mac's map reading, I was "riding shotgun" and my first vision was a Fw 190 perched on top of a Ju 88.'

Roy LeLong described his attack in his combat report: '*I approached the aerodrome from the East, the aerodrome being hard to find owing to snow and ice. On approach, I flew parallel to E-W runway on the South side. At first I could not see any aircraft, but finally saw about 5-6 Fw 190 and Ju 88 pick-a-backs with normal camouflage well dispersed in fir trees. My sight was u/s, so I used the plate glass for sighting, letting strikes hit the ground in front of one of these pick-a-backs. I pulled the nose up a little and saw many strikes on both the Fw and the Ju 88. Numerous personnel working around these E/A were scattered by the attack. I turned South into the next dispersal bay and made a similar type of attack on another pick-a-back, also seeing strikes. I then turned West and attacked for a second time the first pick-a-back which I had previously damaged. This time both the Ju 88 and Fw 190 burst into flames. After breaking away from this last attack, light flak opened up at me, so we headed for our rendezvous at Mariager. Two columns of black smoke were seen long after the aerodrome was left.'*

Seconds later, the second Mosquito made its first run. Tony Craft recalls: 'We were following – "hugging the deck" – young Waters busy looking all around to make sure we were not being jumped. But we were just too low on our first run and missed out…'

Tony Craft wrote after the mission: '*I approached Tirstrup from the East at zero feet. Flew down E-W runway and saw a Ju 88 painted black, to starboard in a wood to the North of the runway. Before turning starboard in an orbit to attack, I saw the Fw 190 and Ju 88 pick-a-back aircraft in flames subsequent to F/O LeLong's attack. I then attacked the Ju 88 from E-W and left it in flames (11.10 hrs). Just after this attack, 3 light guns opened up at us from West of aerodrome.*'

'The strict rule was to "beat it"!'

A Mistel S2 (Fw 190 A or F and a Ju 88 G-1, W.Nr. 714633), 'Red 11', of 6./KG 200 seen close to its woodland dispersal at the edge of Tirstrup airfield in Denmark, spring 1945.

John Waters: 'Tony Craft obviously had a fixation on this black Ju 88 and we were too low to have a go at the "pick-a-back" straight ahead. I think Roy LeLong did three runs and we did two. The Ju 88 would have been nailed on our second run. I can still see those "pick-a-back" aircraft – and our frustration when the bloody guns got stuck (we hardly used any ammunition). I can also still see the ground crews scattering, such was our surprise visit! When the light Flak opened up, I suppose I got scared and too excited that I gave my pilot the ground speed to steer instead of the compass course – true inefficiency in the style of Pilot Officer Prune. The result was the two aircraft left the airfield in opposite directions – which I insist foxed those Hun gunners! But once that Flak started Roy LeLong phoned us up and we quit *immediately*.'

Roy LeLong told a newspaper reporter afterwards. 'When we left, the composite and another plane were blazing furiously. We riddled another composite nearby.' [1]

---

[1]. The two Mosquitoes had raided the *Luftwaffe* unit II./KG 200, stationed at Tirstrup to undertake a proposed *Mistel* operation against the British Fleet at Scapa Flow, code-named *Drachenhöhle*. See: *Mistel, German Composite Aircraft and Operations 1942-1945*, by Robert Forsyth, Classic Publications, London, 2001.

Pilots of the RAF Fighter Experimental Flight line up for a snapshot taken by F/O John Waters on a wintry day at Ford in early 1945. Seen together with the Flight's commander, S/L Bob Kipp, (fifth from left) are three of the four aircrew who took part in the Tirstrup raid on 14 February 1945; F/L Tony Craft (first left), F/O Roy LeLong (sixth from left) and F/O 'Mac' McLaren (third from right). Behind them is the all-silver Mosquito FB. VI belonging to night-fighter ace, Wing Commander John Cunningham, who was visiting the unit at the time.

John Waters: 'We rejoined at the lake at Mariager and returned to base. I have a vivid memory of two men who stopped hoeing in a field – and waved to us – just before we crossed the coast. On arriving home, we taxied to dispersal, stopped the engines, undid our straps, took off our helmets and as I slid out backwards through the door, my pilot let go of the stick which just flopped to one side and lo! – there were two *thuds* as our two wing tanks dropped to the ground! I quickly darted to our dispersal hut to hear two sergeant ground staff receiving what can only be described as a "right good bollocking" and a lot of nasty threats!'

Thus ended a typical day in a Mosquito unit in a long war – a war that had started for this 'wooden wonder' four years previously in late 1941. In that time the aircraft had carved itself an enviable record in operations throughout the conflict, far and wide. But it could have been so different because the 'powers that be', who had so enthusiastically embraced the aircraft once operations commenced in 1941, were in part the very ones who tried to stifle the Mosquito's development in the late 1930s. If it had not been for Geoffrey de Havilland's persistence and his supporters, the Mosquito would never have graced the skies.

'WE'LL DO IT ANYWAY' 2

Left: Three members of the DH Mosquito Design Team not available for the group shot seen on page 2. They are from left to right: A.W. Fawcett, C. C. Jackson; electrics and J. E. Walker; engine installation designer. It was Walker who accompanied Geoffrey de Havilland Jr. on the first and second flights of the Mosquito prototype as an observer – see page 20. (BAE Systems)

THE DH. 98 Mosquito was regarded by many as a first for de Havilland, 'a fast light bomber' that could be said to have had 'family links' to the DH. 4, an aircraft designed by Airco (Aircraft Manufacturing Company) in World War One. The DH.4 was a fast, light, two-seat, single-engine day bomber that was used by many squadrons throughout the RFC and RNAS, first seeing action in early 1917. The initials 'DH' came from Geoffrey de Havilland, the chief designer at Airco at the time. The DH. 4 proved to be an excellent aircraft. It was highly popular with its crews and held the same attractions as its later famous sister – notably ease of operation, high-speed when fully loaded with bombs and general reliability with good altitude performance which prevented enemy fighter interception under favourable conditions.

Another notable link between the two aircraft was in the power plants. Both aircraft used aero engines designed by Rolls-Royce: the R-R Eagle VIII in the DH. 4 and the R-R Merlin in the Mosquito. The DH. 4 used a variety of engine types but it was the Eagle that gave it the performance where it excelled and it was the same company's ubiquitous Merlin that made the Mosquito the success it was. One can imagine the position of Britain in the late 1930s if Rolls-Royce had not privately developed the Merlin. Where would the Spitfire and Hurricane have been in 1940 without it, not to mention the later succession of Allied types that it powered?

D.H. "COMET"

Genesis: The DH. 88 and DH. 91

The De Havilland Aircraft Company was created in 1920, when Airco's assets were sold to BSA (Birmingham Small Arms) by George Holt Thomas, the owner of Airco. BSA was not interested in pursuing aviation so Geoffrey de Havilland, wanting to continue in aviation design and manufacturing, bought the aviation-related assets and set up the company under his own name at Stag Lane Aerodrome, Edgware, West London. However, at the outbreak of the war, the company was situated at Hatfield in Hertfordshire, north of London. It was at this site, and the nearby Salisbury Hall, that the story of the Mosquito began.

Into this story is woven the influence of two other De Havilland designs: the DH. 88 Comet and the DH. 91 Albatross. In 1930, the question of how the Australian state of Victoria and its capital city of Melbourne might celebrate their coming centenary produced a suggestion from Melbourne's Lord Mayor, Harold Smith, that an air race linking England with Australia be organised. A sponsor was sought and found in the person of wealthy confectionery manufacturer, Sir Macpherson Robertson, of MacRobertson's Chocolates, and so the great 1934 London to Melbourne MacRobertson Air Race was born. The air race was to have many long overland stages and for this the De Havilland company, in a spirit of national unity, produced a design for a twin engine, wooden, two-seat aircraft capable of achieving 200 mph over a range of 3,000 miles. The result was the DH. 88 Comet. The design and appearance

Right: The original 'Mosquito' – the DH. 4 of 1917. A light bomber that shared many of the attributes of its later sister: ease of operations, high-speed when fully armed with bombs and good altitude performance which prevented fighter interception due to its relative high speed.

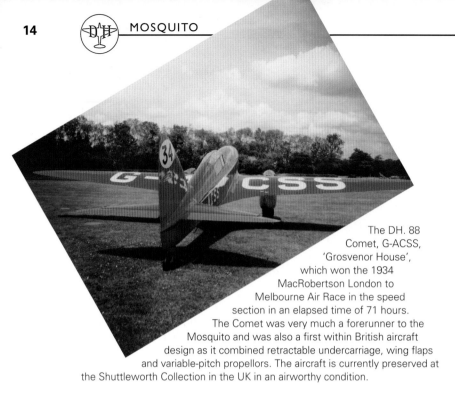

The DH. 88
Comet, G-ACSS,
'Grosvenor House',
which won the 1934
MacRobertson London to
Melbourne Air Race in the speed
section in an elapsed time of 71 hours.
The Comet was very much a forerunner to the
Mosquito and was also a first within British aircraft
design as it combined retractable undercarriage, wing flaps
and variable-pitch propellors. The aircraft is currently preserved at
the Shuttleworth Collection in the UK in an airworthy condition.

The beautiful and elegant all wood DH. 91 Frobisher Class Albatross prototype, G-AEVV, the aircraft first flew on 20 May 1937. Originally conceived as a fast transatlantic mailplane (two were built named – 'Faraday' (above) and 'Franklin'), it was soon made into a successful airliner in its own right. Five versions were built carrying 22 passengers, these were named 'Frobisher', 'Falcon', 'Fortuna', 'Fingal' and 'Fiona'. Interestingly when DH was designing the later Mosquito, the DH. 91 formed the basis of the initial design proposals. G-AEVV was later transferred from Imperial Airways to BOAC when it was formed in 1940, but in turn ended up serving with No. 271 Squadron RAF. It was destroyed in a landing accident at Reykjavik on 11 August 1941.

was a forerunner of the later Mosquito, featuring all-wooden construction contained within a very streamlined fuselage and powered by two up-rated Gipsy Six engines. Three Comets were built: G-ACSP, G-ACSR and G-ACSS. One of these, G-ACSS, with the race number '34' and carrying the name 'Grosvenor House' in a scarlet finish, went on to win the race in the speed section for Britain in an elapsed time of 71 hours, 1 minute, 3 seconds. It is interesting to note that, at the time of the design of the Comet, it is said that de Havilland had offered a high-speed bomber version of the Comet to the Air Ministry, but it was declined.

The other DH design, which had a more fundamental influence over the later Mosquito, was the DH. 91 Albatross airliner. Designed in 1936 to an Air Ministry specification 36/35 for a transatlantic mailplane, its capability as an airliner was not lost and a version carrying 22 passengers was designed, five of which were eventually built and used by Imperial Airways and later BOAC. The Albatross was the first to use the ply-balsa-ply method of sandwich construction in the fuselage and large wooden sections in the wing that were to be utilized in the construction of the Mosquito. The clean and very elegant Albatross was capable of cruising at 210 mph (338 km/h) at 11,000 ft (3,350 m) on its four Gipsy Six engines.

Early Development

In 1936 Geoffrey de Havilland became interested in pursuing possible work with the Air Ministry (AM). There were many within the government and the military who were becoming increasingly concerned about the growing rearmament in Germany and this was not lost within the boardrooms of many aviation companies. De Havilland was not alone; Supermarine and Hawker were also pursuing modern monoplane fighter designs. Technologically, the RAF at the time was woefully behind compared to the emerging *Luftwaffe*, with front line fighter types still in the biplane era and bomber designs not much more advanced.

De Havilland had had some experience with the Air Ministry and government specifications in the 1920s and, in light of current political feelings, took an interest in specification P.13/36 issued on 24 August 1936. This specification called for a twin-engine bomber capable of flying for 1,000 miles at 275 mph at 15,000 feet with a 1,000-pound bomb load. The idea was to combine medium bomber, general reconnaissance and general purpose activities in one basic design with nose and tail turrets. De Havilland was unimpressed with the specification, stating that the performance could not be met with

Above: A young Geoffrey de Havilland at the controls of his second design, the DH. Biplane No.2 in 1910 and below in a post-war portrait. He was a driving force behind the Mosquito, especially in the corridors of power where the concept of an unarmed bomber was met with incredulity. His company was to go on to produce a high number of hugely successful aircraft including the DH. 82 Tiger Moth, DH. 89 Dragon Rapide, DH. 100 Vampire, DH. 106 Comet, DH. 114 Heron and the DH. (Hawker) 125 to name but a few. (via Stephen Skinner)

an armed, metal twin-engine aircraft. The Ministry, however, had other ideas.

Both Avro and Handley Page answered the brief with, respectively, the Manchester and the Halifax (the Halifax was originally designed as a twin-engine bomber) but both were flawed fundamentally due to the specification itself. De Havilland felt that speed was paramount and thoughts turned to a smaller, lighter airframe. Because of this, de Havilland issued a design based around a modified Albatross, powered by the forthcoming new Merlin engine, though with a lighter bomb load to retain high performance. With an all-wooden construction based on the same production methods used in the Albatross, the twin-engine bomber was designed to outrun pursuing fighters, so negating the need for defensive armament. The design was rejected in many quarters as, at this time, the RAF had a policy that a bomber needed to be heavy and well armed so that it could battle its way into and out of a target; the theory being that '… the bomber would always get through.' This accepted thinking produced the types then coming into operation: Wellingtons, Hampdens, Whitleys and Blenheims – all heavy, relatively slow and armed with turrets.

By 1938, with the Munich Crisis in full swing, de Havilland was still toying with the P.13/36 proposal and looked again at a twin Merlin Albatross though, by now, the company could see that even this was not working well due to the power-to-weight ratio. It still championed the fast, unarmed bomber but knew that, in order to work, it would need to be a smaller airframe than the Albatross-based design, again powered by two Merlins and with a crew of only two. The seed had been sown. However, by this time, Geoffrey de Havilland was increasingly concerned about the disinterest being placed on his concept. After one unsuccessful meeting at the Air Ministry, de Havilland turned to C. C. Walker (Chief Engineer) as they drove back to Hatfield and said, *'We'll do it anyway.'* Fortunately he had an ally in the Air Council in the form of Air Marshal Wilfred Freeman whom he had known since the First World War. Freeman who had been head of Research and Development since 1936 believed in de Havilland's concept and became an important advocate for DH in the corridors of power. In some circles de Havilland's concept became known as 'Freeman's Folly'.

With 1939 came an increasing urgency for Britain's rearmament as the mood on the streets and in Whitehall was one of impending war with Germany. Yet DH was still facing indifference to its concept for a fast unarmed bomber. The conventional metal bomber at the time, fitted with powered turrets and hand-held weapons, was penalised by the weight of the structure and the fuel needed to carry them, which would make it vulnerable to Flak and fighters. What was really required were the elements of high speed, height and manoeuvrability to allow bombers to evade fighters and Flak. The larger metal aircraft took longer to build, to man, to maintain and to operate. The smaller design would be easier and cheaper to build, require fewer crew with less time over the target and could be turned around faster for more operations.

However, at the time of Britain's declaration of war on 3 September 1939, following Germany's invasion of Poland, DH's unarmed concept was still making little headway. On 6 September de Havilland approached the Ministry again and, whilst the clouds of war made the men at the Ministry a little more receptive, they were still very skeptical about the performance figures given for the unarmed bomber in operational service. The Ministry was also insisting on some form of defensive armament; it wanted a powered turret, which meant a third crew member. Several paper developments using different engine types were studied, all with the turret fitted, but all showed that there was a corresponding weight and performance penalty. Because of its current availability and future potential, the Merlin was by far the best option but the turret was still an issue for the Air Ministry. For turreted versus unarmed aircraft, the cruising speeds were 279 vs 325 mph, and the maximum speeds were 355 vs 409 mph, but the Ministry was unmoved.

At a meeting on 22 November 1939, Sir Wilfred Freeman reviewed the development findings from DH and fortunately championed the corner for the removal of the turret. Discussions also centred upon reconnaissance and a possible long-range four-cannon fighter; R. E. Bishop, the Chief Designer, was already thinking ahead. The performance figures for the DH. 98, as it was then called, were found to be promising; they were slightly better than the Spitfire, then Britain's front-line military fighter. Estimated figures showed that the DH. 98 was some 20 mph faster even carrying 1,000 lbs of bombs. 12 December saw a high-level meeting with Bomber Command, Research and Development personnel, the Assistant Chief of the Air Staff and other interested parties. The project continued to face an uphill struggle, as the concept of an unarmed bomber was still too foreign, but there was one positive outcome: they agreed on the concept of unarmed reconnaissance. The DH. 98 had been thrown a lifeline.

As ever, Sir Wilfred Freeman, who always believed in de Havilland, strongly backed the unarmed concept and a decision was made to order a prototype, with emphasis on the reconnaissance role, with bomber and fighter types to be investigated. Design staff were quickly assembled and it was decreed that, in order to avoid possible air attack at Hatfield, the design team should move to an old moated house. This was Salisbury Hall, a few miles east of Hatfield, near London Colney. The design team there was headed by R.E. Bishop and in the grounds of the house a hangar, disguised as a barn, was erected in which to build the prototype. On 1 March 1940, contract 69990/40 was issued stipulating that 50 bomber/reconnaissance aircraft, including the prototype, were to be built to Specification B.1/40. Development design work proceeded with haste, a mock-up taking shape during the Battle of France.

With the fall of Paris and Dunkirk, and Churchill's speech in which he declared of the enemy, *'We shall fight them on the beaches…'*, echoing through Parliament and the sitting rooms of England, pressure was put on de Havilland to suspend all further work on the Mosquito. The country's need was for all energies to be diverted to manufacturing existing aircraft types. Lord Beaverbrook, Minister of Aircraft Production, told Freeman to stop work on the Mosquito. He felt that there would be no Mosquitoes ready operationally by early 1941 if development continued. This and the increasing nationwide pressure on materials, along with the commencement of the Battle of Britain in July, forced a suspension of work at Salisbury

Hall. De Havilland was facing an uphill battle with Beaverbrook and it took a personal discussion with him to explain the Mosquito's low demands on existing production methods due to its non-strategic material usage and engineering design. To keep the project alive, de Havilland had to promise 50 Mosquitoes by July 1941! The company won the day, but only just – 50 by July was a tall order.

Throughout the Battle of Britain, work continued on the prototype, with a real sense that a lot was at stake for the country and for the Mosquito itself: Hatfield and surrounding districts were not spared the harsh realities of *Luftwaffe* bombing. The most direct hit was made by a lone Junkers Ju 88 A4 from *Stab* 1./KG 77 which, on 3 October, being denied its original target due to inclement weather, found Hatfield by chance. It made a number of runs across the facility, machine-gunning and dropping four bombs that killed 21 people and destroyed a large quantity of raw material assigned to the Mosquito project. The Ju 88 was subsequently shot down.

On 3 November 1940 the completed prototype (now disassembled at Salisbury Hall) was taken by 'Queen Mary' trailer to Hatfield for reassembly, resplendent in an all-over yellow colour scheme. The Mosquito, carrying the 'B Condition' serial E0234, commenced engine runs in early November, 11 months after start of design work. Taxiing trials continued on 24 November and on the following day,

Above: The first of many: the Mosquito prototype is seen after both Merlins were fitted in the hangar in which the aircraft was designed and built, and which was disguised as a barn in the grounds of Salisbury Hall (far left) in September 1940. The prototype was powered by Merlin 21s rated at 1,280 hp on take-off. Note the blisters on the side of the canopy and the simple six-into-one exhaust system, which was to cause many problems until it was radically redesigned into a conventional system. (BAE Systems)

After completion at Salisbury Hall, the prototype was dismantled and trucked the few miles to Hatfield on 'Queen Mary' trailers on 3 November 1940 (above), where it was reassembled and where final checks and engine runs commenced. It has to be said there was some difficulty in reassembling the aircraft: 'Things didn't seem to fit as well as they had down at Salisbury Hall,' recalled Rex King from the design and development team. The tarpaulins are covering the all-yellow aircraft in a bid to avoid detection by the Luftwaffe. In the air the all-yellow scheme was to warn anti-aircraft gunners and RAF fighter pilots that the aircraft was a prototype. The aircraft is seen outside the old Tiger Moth paint shop at Hatfield – the only space available on the aerodrome for the prototype. It became known as the 'Mosquito home'.
(BAE Systems)

Geoffrey de Havilland Jr made a short 'hop', followed later in the afternoon by a half-hour flight with John Walker as observer. Born on a cold and overcast November day, this was one of the most remarkable aircraft to come out of the world conflict and, undeniably, one of the most beautiful aircraft to grace the skies, before or since.

By December 1940 the Battle of Britain had been fought and won, but Britain stood alone with the night *Blitz* affecting the home front. The gloomy news on the war front reflected the weather in the early part of the year – grey and drizzly. However, by 19 February 1941 the prototype, serialled W4050, had made 50 flights and all who saw her, including her doubting detractors, were most impressed with her performance. It was at this stage that thoughts turned to possible manufacture in Canada and a fighter version. It was decided that 150 more Mosquitoes were to be ordered from Canada, with the existing British contract 69990 reduced to 19 reconnaissance and 28 fighters and with bombers to figure in the next 150 ordered.

The prototype suffered a potential setback on 24 February 1941 whilst taxiing across a bumpy airfield at Boscombe Down. The castoring tail wheel jammed and it was subsequently found that the rear fuselage had fractured aft of the trailing edge. The castoring of the tail wheel had been an ongoing problem for the design team. It was now felt that this problem could doom the aircraft. However,

such was the enthusiasm for the aircraft at higher levels that there was little concern and very soon de Havilland had dispatched the PR prototype fuselage (originally for W4051) to Boscombe Down and this was fitted within a few days. Flying commenced on 14 March. The greatest concern facing the aircraft's handling was tailplane flutter but, through many tests using several trialling methods, the problem was cured by extending the rear of the engine nacelles aft of the trailing edge of the wing, necessitating splitting of the flaps either side of the nacelle. These extended nacelles were fitted over the existing ones after 14 March, in time for recommencement of flying at Boscombe Down.

The prototype became the principal airframe for much experimental flying, in particular for developments within the bomber series, and included a mock-up four-gun turret fitted on 24 July. In October 1941, two-stage Merlin 61s were fitted to the prototype and it attained 40,000 feet with these on 20 June 1942. W4050 then had Merlin 77s fitted and in November 1942 she attained the highest speed ever reached by any Mosquito: 437 mph (some records state 439 mph). Flying continued into 1943 with a short period on loan to Rolls-Royce and taking part in a film about the Mosquito. She was finally grounded in early 1944.

Below: An army of technicians with the prototype at Hatfield on 19 November 1940, performing fuel flows and engine checks. Note the absent undercarriage doors. The prototype initially carried the 'B Condition' serial E0234 for the initial testing. Interestingly the prototype had Handley Page leading edge slots fitted, but these were soon seen as not necessary and were locked before the first flight. They are still fitted to the prototype to this day. (BAE Systems)

Above: Another view from 19 November 1940. The port cowlings have now been replaced and an engine run is being undertaken – though the starboard lower cowling is still not fitted as it can be seen on the grass. Note the pilot walking past the tailplane (which is being held down during the engine runs); he is undoubtedly walking to the Tiger Moth parked behind. (BAE Systems)

Right: 21 November 1940: The prototype is pushed out for more engine and taxiing runs at Hatfield. (BAE Systems)

25 November 1940, 3.45pm – history in the making, with the first flight of the prototype Mosquito at Hatfield on an overcast afternoon eleven months after commencement of design.
At the controls for the 30-minute flight was Geoffrey de Havilland Jr. and John E. Walker as observer. Paradoxically Geoffrey de Havilland Jr. referred to the aircraft as 'the boiler', a term of affection. From her third flight she gained the military serial W4050. On 24 February the prototype's fuselage was fractured whilst taxiing at Boscombe Down due to faulty tail wheel castoring – this necessitated the fuselage being replaced with the one destined for W4051, the prototype PR version. In March 1941 the prototype underwent an 'Initial Handling Report' at Boscombe Down and the results were extremely encouraging on most accounts. The report was received at Hatfield as 'a most favourable and heartening document', a real vindication for the design. By 14 April 1941 the prototype had made 100 flights. (BAE Systems)

Left: A by now camouflaged W4050 seen on 2 September 1942 (still with yellow undersides) with two-stage two-speed Merlin 61s fitted. She flew with these engines from October 1941 and reached a speed of 432 mph on 23 July 1942. From 8 October 1942 to 1 July 1943, she was fitted with Merlin 77s and made 23 flights attaining the highest speed by any Mosquito: 437 mph (some records state 439 mph). These tests were crucial as they paved the way for the introduction of the two-stage Merlin into Mosquito production. Standing on the left is John de Havilland, a test pilot (like his brother Geoffrey de Havilland Jr and Peter de Havilland). Sadly, John and Geoffrey were to both lose their lives – John in a collision with another Mosquito near St. Albans on 23 August 1943 and Geoffrey in the break-up and crash of the DH.108, TG306 on 27 September 1946. It is interesting to note that W4050, which is currently preserved at Salisbury Hall is to be restored with two-stage Merlin 70 series engines, replicating her appearance in 1942-43. (BAE Systems)

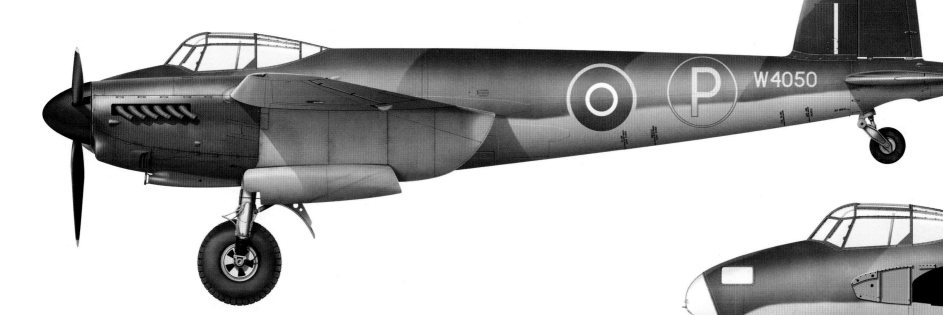

Prototype Mosquito W4050 as she appeared in late 1942 to mid 1943, when powered with Merlin 77s
Note the two longitudinal repair 'patches' on the fuselage to the left of the roundel, acquired during the prototypes second fuselage fracture on 18 May 1941. The fuselage was damaged on the port side aft of the trailing edge at Boscombe Down by a heavy landing during overload tests. Unlike the earlier fracture of 24 February 1941, which saw the fuselage being replaced, the fuselage was repaired at Hatfield. These repairs can be seen to this day on the preserved prototype.

'DON'T SPARE THE GLUE' 3

Right: Canadian production of the Mosquito commenced with a 'prototype' - a bomber B. VII, (essentially the British-built B. IV). This aircraft, KB300 first flew on 24 September 1942, under the capable hands of Ralph Spradbrow, chief test pilot at Downsview. The 'B. VII' was a provisional term for this aircraft – it later became the B. XX in production, powered by Packard Merlin 31s or 33s. Here are two factory fresh Canadian B. XXVs – essentially B. XXs powered by Packard Merlin 225s. 400 B. XXVs were built at Downsview, 343 of which served with the RAF. KB424 is having engine checks made – note the upper cowling removed from the port Merlin and the lower cowling from the starboard Merlin. This Mosquito was ferried across the Atlantic to the UK by the very capable RAF Ferry Command and saw service with No. 608 and 162 Squadrons in the Light Night Striking Force role before being SOC on 6 December 1945. KB428 behind, remained in Canada with the RCAF.

Left: T. IIIs under assembly at Leavesden in Britain in June 1943. A number of these Mosquitoes were later converted to NF. XVIIs by Marshalls in Cambridge. Some of the identified Mosquitoes in the original photograph which became NF. XVIIs are: HK287, joined 125 Squadron, belly-landed Coltishall 5 May 1945; HK 289, joined 219 Squadron, then passed to 68 Squadron, shot down by own AA fire near Somerley, Suffolk, 14 November 1944; HK290, joined 456 Squadron, SOC 19 June 1945; HK292, joined 219 Squadron and went missing on 20 June 1944, assumed crashed in North Sea. (BAE Systems)

Built in Three Countries

THE Mosquito was unique in that not only was it built in the UK, (5,570 built during the war), but also in Canada and Australia. Even before the war began it was recognised that the de Havilland plant at Downsview in Toronto had the capacity to produce more aircraft; why not Mosquitoes? Such was the need for Mosquitoes that Hatfield was being pressed to produce 150 Mosquitoes per month and the proposed 40 plus that Downsview could produce per month were a welcome addition to the RAF and RCAF.

Getting a complex aircraft like the Mosquito off the drawing board and on to a production line was a challenging process, necessitating much work, ingenuity and, initially, using a good number of Hatfield staff to assist and speed the process. The Canadians were not short of ideas, devising new methods in the construction process such as concrete moulds in place of the conventional timber variety, infrared fuselage drying and a very streamlined assembly process at the Downsview plant. The initial emphasis in Canada was to be on the bomber version. Here it was initially called the B. Mk.VII and the first Downsview-built Mosquito, KB300, took to the air on 24 September 1942. By March 1945, 80 Mosquitoes had been built that month alone, making a total of 728. At the time of the cessation of hostilities in Europe in May, 887 had been produced at Downsview. Of these, 430 bombers and 59 fighter-bombers were serving in Europe. By October 1945, 1,032 Mosquitoes had been completed in Canada.

Australia held the distinction of having the oldest overseas de Havilland subsidiary outside Britain, established in March 1927 in Melbourne. DHA (de Havilland Australia) relocated to Sydney in 1930 at Mascot. In November 1940, serious thought was given at the plant to building military aircraft for operational service and a report was submitted to the Government. The biggest issue until that time had been the supply of larger components from the UK, especially engines, over such a large distance in a world at war. In the US, Packard's undertaking to produce the Merlin under licence aided Canada's decision to make the Mosquito and in turn Australia's decision to produce not only the Mosquito, but also the P-51D Mustang, which was built in Australia by C.A.C. (Commonwealth Aircraft Corporation) in Melbourne.

In March 1942 the Australian Government asked the de Havilland Sydney plant to produce the FB.VI for service with the RAAF. To aid this an F. Mk. II, DD664, was disassembled and shipped out from the UK. The greatest hurdle was the multitude of drawings, components, jigs and materials that the aircraft needed, but in addition subcontractors had to be found and skilled staff trained. Much assistance was provided by Hatfield and Downsview and by December 1942, DD664 was assembled and flying and, by March 1943, a pair of Packard Merlin 31s (replacing the UK-made Merlins) was installed and the aircraft gained an Australian serial, A52-1001.

The first Australian-made Mosquito, an FB. Mk. 40, serial A52-1 (essentially an FB.VI with Packard Merlins) took off on its maiden flight on 23 July 1943. But production was hampered in Australia by a multitude of issues including component and skill shortages, slow receipt of parts from overseas, lack of assembly jigs, machine tools and engines, and poor quality cold-drawn nickel steel. All these factors, and more, conspired to set back the delivery schedule seriously. On top of this were a number of fatal wing failures in flight which, although attributed to excess flight loads, led to examinations of the wings supplied by the subcontractor, General Motors Holden. Some showed poor construction and all Australian-made Mosquito aircraft were grounded in July 1944. By 31 May 1945 all these issues had been resolved and 75 aircraft had been constructed. By 15 August this had increased to 108 with the grand total at a modest 225

Right: A wartime Australian wind-tunnel model of a Mosquito FB. Mk. 40 (FB. VI).
(Australian Aviation Museum, Bankstown)

delivered to the RAAF at the close of production in 1948, by then with virtually the whole aircraft being Australian-made.

Unlike the Canadian product, all Mosquitoes built in Australia were for home-based RAAF use, supplemented by UK-supplied FB.VIs, T. IIIs and PR. XVIs. Production was not just limited to the FB. 40 and the need for photo-reconnaissance created the PR. 40, a production line conversion of the fighter-bomber to carry cameras. Unarmed, these aircraft carried a vertically mounted camera in the nose in place of the .303s and two more cameras aft, with the addition of two oblique cameras. Post-war development of the Australian PR Mosquitoes saw the introduction of the PR. 41 (two-stage Merlin 69s) which replaced the UK-supplied PR. XVIs used in the aerial mapping of Australia. 22 FB. Mk. 40s were also converted to dual-control trainers, known as T. Mk. 43s. At least one of these trainers retained its armament.

Wartime Production Totals	
UK	5,570
CANADA	1,032
AUSTRALIA	108
TOTALS	**6,710**

Total Production including	
post-war	**7,781**

Including UK prototypes and Canadian and Australian Mosquito derivatives – there were some 64 different marks of Mosquito.

Right: The first Mosquito to be built in Australia was an FB. Mk. 40 (FB. VI), serial A52-1. It is seen here in the background in an all-aluminium finish (apart from the fin and rudder which was camouflaged) and first flew on 23 July 1943 with DH test pilot, W/C Gibson Lee, at the controls. The Mosquito in the foreground is a UK-supplied T. III. A52-1 was delivered to the RAAF on 4 March 1944 and was destroyed when an air bottle burst whilst being charged on 14 June 1944, wrecking the fuselage. Note that the (Packard) Merlins used in A52-1 have six exhaust stubs as against the five (six into five) in most UK-built T. III, NF/F. IIs and FB. VI examples.

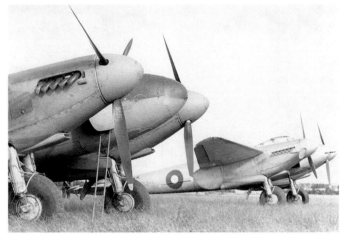

A wartime DH advertisement emphasising the part played by Canadian-built Mosquitoes in bolstering the Allied war effort.

Right: Fuselages under construction in the UK over mahogany moulds. The sign at the back stresses the importance of what the workers are doing: 'Mistakes on aircraft may lead to loss of life. Will operators please report any errors to the Foreman or Inspection Dept.' It has to be said that at the time Mosquito production began there were 12,000 skilled woodworkers unemployed in the UK alone – thus a vital contribution was made by a work force then underutilised in the conflict. The mould in the foreground is for the port fuselage shell, the one behind is the starboard. The moulds here would appear to be for the armed fighter type Mosquito and derivatives. Amongst the companies making fuselage shells in the UK was: E. Gomme and Styles & Mealing at High Wycombe and Walter Lawrence at Sawbridgeworth. (BAE Systems)

The Mosquito described

After the Comet and the Albatross, the Mosquito was to be the last De Havilland aircraft built almost entirely of wood. In a world increasingly given over to metal aircraft, De Havilland was the accepted master of this construction. The Mosquito fuselage was an oval, tapering cross-section, built entirely in two halves, much like a model aircraft kit. It was a stiff but relatively light monocoque (or stressed skin construction) created in two longitudinal sections by using two layers of plywood sheeting glued together with a balsa wood filler, internal wooden stiffeners and integrated bulkheads. These structures (port and starboard) were created over two mahogany (or concrete) moulds, which conformed to the interior shape of the fuselage. The inner and outer plywood skins of three-ply birch ranged from 1.5 to 2 mm in thickness. In each stage of the ply-balsa-ply construction the structure was secured over the mould by broad flexible steel-band cramps, which were tightened by turnbuckles to give the required pressure for bonding the ply-balsa-ply with the glue.

Once dry, the two half shells were lifted out from their moulds and prepared for the fitting of around 60 per cent of the aircraft's internal equipment in each half. The two half-fuselages were then glued together, or 'boxed-up' as it was known. Once assembled the remainder of the internal equipment was fitted, along with the canopy. This form of construction greatly speeded up the assembly process as it allowed greater access by all parties in the fitting-out stage. Once joined up, the outer surface was covered in Irish linen and mandapolam material, applied with a red tautening dope and, finally painted.

The wing was a one-piece cantilevered wooden construction built wing-tip to wing-tip and containing two box spars stressed to carry 82 tons (fighter-bomber). Stressed plywood skin (reinforced by

The glue that held a Mosquito together. The glue used by DH was originally Casein, a milk based adhesive, but it was found it encouraged fungus under certain environmental conditions. It was replaced by synthetic "Beetle", invented by Aero Research at Duxford. It was introduced around 1942 and was resistant to humidity and to the temperature cycling of Mosquitoes operating in the tropics to wintery European airfields. Tests showed that the wood fibres tore before the Beetle glue gave way. Beetle was in turn replaced by Redux, a glue used on the Mosquitoes baby brother, the DH 103 Hornet – see page 128.

Bomber fuselages under construction in Canada. 1. Fitting bulkheads, reinforcing members and longitudinal members that carry the wings into the (Canadian invented) concrete moulds. **2.** Fuselage mould showing at left, inserts for collars and wing connections and right, single inner ply held in place by steel strapping (cramps) under tension. All openings were constructed integrally, to be cut out later. **3.** The inner fuselage skin has been fitted and the between-skin structural stiffeners are being laid prior to the balsa infill and final outer fuselage skin. The rear fuselage veneers were laid diagonally to counter torque. **4.** Pressure is applied to the outer skin of laminated birch by cramps to compress the whole ply-balsa-ply into one solid half-fuselage section. **5.** After the glue has set, the cramps are released and the half-fuselage is lifted from the mould. **6.** Half-fuselage sections; brackets and bulkheads are in place, and around 60 per cent of internal equipment is then fitted before the fuselages are 'boxed-up' (joined up).

Above: British-manufactured fighter-bomber fuselages in 1943 prior to being 'boxed-up' (background) with a fuselage in the foreground nearly completed prior to being doped and painted. Note the paper covered canopy being fitted – these were produced in UK by Courtney Pope of London and Perfecta Motors of Birmingham.

Australian FB. Mk. 40 fuselages undergoing fitting out in Annandale in Sydney. De Havilland took over the piano factory of Beale and Co Ltd to produce this part of the aircraft. A variety of Sydney furniture factories produced other components: Rickets and Thorp Pty Ltd, front spar; F Dickin Pty Ltd, rear spar; Bray and Halliday Pty Ltd, wing skins; Reilton and Griffin, tank doors. (Australian Aviation Museum, Bankstown)

internal span–wise wooden stringers) covered the wing surface. Ten self-sealing fuel tanks were installed within the wing, accessed by removable panels on the lower surface. Wood screws were used throughout the construction process and were screwed in whilst the glue was wet. If there was one requirement for the work force during the construction process of the Mosquito it was *'Don't spare the glue!'*

The completed wing containing its split, plywood inner flaps and outer metal ailerons was mated to the fuselage by four main bolts and by additional bolts passing through the flanges of the inner ribs. Like the fuselage, it too was covered in Irish linen and mandapolam. The tailplane and fin used a box structure, covered again in plywood skins. Internally the rudder and elevators were made of metal 'Alclad' with a fabric covering on the rudder and metal covering on the elevators: the elevators were originally fabric covered, but service use by the RAF and BOAC necessitated them being covered in metal.

The Merlin engines were mounted on welded steel tube frames bolted to the wing front spar and upper undercarriage fixed structure. The oil and coolant radiators for each engine were built into the leading edge between the engine nacelle and the fuselage. The two engine nacelles were in metal and fully streamlined. They enclosed the fully retractable main undercarriage. The tail wheel was also retractable. The main undercarriage was unique in its design, avoiding the need to manufacture the conventional oleo–pneumatic leg by replacing it with an outer metal case of two folded halves of sheet metal containing eleven and a half rubber blocks in compression – these undercarriage units were interchangeable.

Contrary to popular belief at the time, the wooden construction in the Mosquito behaved very differently when damaged in combat, actually bringing the aircraft home on many occasions when its conventional metal sisters perished. In a heavy crash-landing it could absorb considerable impact forces, often disintegrating around the crew, whereby they escaped serious injury, often just 'stepping out'. A classic example of the aircraft's strength was given following a port engine failure on take-off to a 139 Squadron Mosquito, crewed by FO Humphrey and F/Sgt Moore of 105 Squadron (the squadrons often shared aircraft) on 26 July 1943. Humphrey recalled: *'It was just over the boundary from the airfield. The engine stopped, and the only thing*

THE ROLLS-ROYCE MERLIN

If there was one other single ingredient in the success of the Mosquito, it would have to be the Rolls-Royce Merlin aero engine. For without this engine and its subsequent derivatives the aircraft would probably not have existed.

The Merlin is a liquid-cooled, 27 litre (1,650 cu in) capacity, V-12 piston aero engine, designed and built by Rolls-Royce Limited. Rolls-Royce named the engine the Merlin after a small European falcon (Falco columbarius). This followed the company convention of naming its piston aero engines after birds of prey.

First run in 1933 and initially known as the PV-12, ('PV' for *private venture* as the company received no government funding) a series of rapidly applied developments, brought about by wartime needs, improved performance markedly.

One of the most notable developments was in the area of supercharging with the introduction of the two-stage, two-speed Merlin first seen in the Mosquito B. Mk VIII and PR. VIII.

Some 14 different variants of the Merlin were developed – with production being undertaken in the UK and under licence in the US by Packard. Canadian- and Australian-produced Mosquitoes used Packard-built Merlins.

Merlin 21
(powered early production Mosquitoes)

Bore - - - - - - - 5.4 in. Capacity 1,649 cu. in. (27 litres)
Stroke - - - - - - 6.0 in. Max. power - - - 1,250 bhp

Australian wings under construction by the sub-contractor General Motors Holden at their plant in Pagewood, Sydney, for FB. Mk. 40 fighter-bombers. Final assembly of Mosquitoes at the DH assembly plant at Bankstown airport in Sydney was halted after some wing construction issues were found which necessitated the grounding of all Australian made Mosquitoes in July 1944. This was eventually resolved and all Australian built Mosquitoes had fit and productive lives well into the mid 1950s when they were retired.

Canadian bomber Mosquitoes undergoing final assembly at the DH assembly plant at Downsview, Toronto. The Canadians developed a very streamlined assembly process at the plant.

British production of bombers. At right, the completed and red doped fuselage has been mated with its wing, fin and canopy. Next will be the fitting of the wing-mounted radiators followed by the undercarriage nacelle, engine fire-wall and Merlin engines. (BAE Systems)

Below: Nearly completed bombers receiving their Merlin engines and cowlings, possibly at Hatfield, 27 April 1943. (BAE Systems)

to do in such circumstances is to shut down and go straight ahead. I remember quite distinctly, I was about 80 to 90 knots and one thinks one did it nice and coolly, but one is talking literally about a split-second decision, and I just shut everything down and pulled the undercarriage up. We were all right. We went charging along for about a mile and went straight through a stone wall and came out all right. You were in a very strong box in a Mosquito, with two engines stuck out each side and in front of you. The main spar was behind you and you had a very strong little place to be in if you hit something straight in front of you, and so we survived going through the wall. Well, everything came to pieces and one shook oneself, but there wasn't any aeroplane, it had broken up.'[1]

It was the pilot's shortest flight on record – 15 seconds.

Importantly, the wooden Mosquito used a good number of nationwide industries that were underused during wartime, notably the various timber trades and associated industries, including motor vehicle coach-builders and machine shops. In all, the manufacture of the various components that made up a Mosquito resulted in the successful subcontracting of approximately 222 individual firms in the UK alone.

---

[1]. *Mosquito Thunder, No. 105 Squadron RAF at War 1942-45*, Stuart R. Scott, Sutton Publishing, Gloucestershire, 1999.

Right: A rare survivor of Australian production of the Mosquito. A detailed descriptive manual on all aspects of the FB. Mk. 40, (using Packard 31 or 33 engines) including flying notes (and the fold-out cut-away on the opposite page), prepared by De Havilland Australia. RAAF Publication No. 390, January 1945.

Left: Newly completed RAAF FB. Mk. 40 fuselages awaiting wings at the DH assembly plant at Bankstown in Sydney. Five can be identified – A52-39, A52-40, A52-42, A52-43, A52-44. Three of these were eventually to be converted to T. Mk. 43s (Trainers) gaining new serials, whilst A52-43 was sold in 1950. A52-40 crashed into the sea off the coast of New South Wales on 16 November 1944. (Australian Aviation Museum, Bankstown)

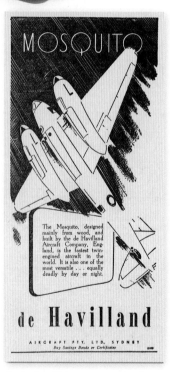

Australian DH company advert. (Stephen Lewis)

Left: Newly completed FB. Mk. 40s undergoing final assembly and inspection in Sydney. Note the two different styles of camouflage. (Australian Aviation Museum, Bankstown)

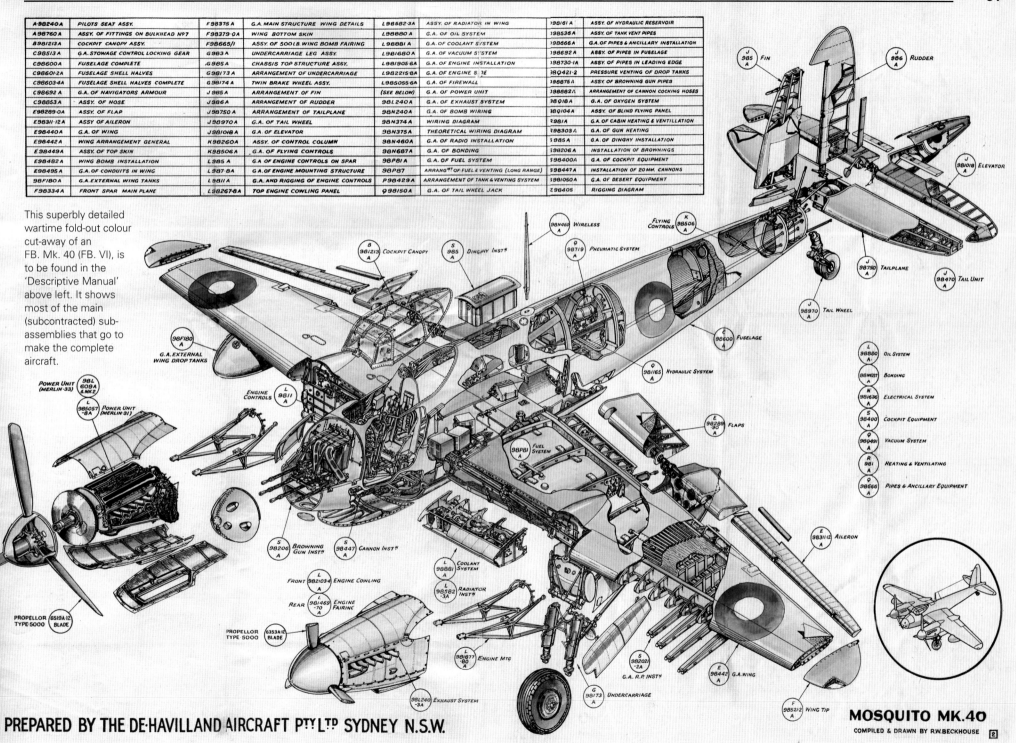

A·98240A	PILOTS SEAT ASSY.	F98375A	G.A. MAIN STRUCTURE WING DETAILS	L98582·3A	ASSY. OF RADIATOR IN WING	98161A	ASSY. OF HYDRAULIC RESERVOIR

Table of sub-assemblies (four columns of part number / description):

A·98240A	PILOTS SEAT ASSY.	F98375A	G.A. MAIN STRUCTURE WING DETAILS	L98582·3A	ASSY. OF RADIATOR IN WING	98161A	ASSY. OF HYDRAULIC RESERVOIR
A98760A	ASSY. OF FITTINGS ON BULKHEAD Nº7	F98379·0A	WING BOTTOM SKIN	L98880A	G.A. OF OIL SYSTEM	98536A	ASSY. OF TANK VENT PIPES
B981213A	COCKPIT CANOPY ASSY.	F98665/1	ASSY. OF 500LB. WING BOMB FAIRING	L98881A	G.A. OF COOLANT SYSTEM	98666A	G.A. OF PIPES & ANCILLARY INSTALLATION
C98513A	G.A. STOWAGE CONTROL LOCKING GEAR	G983A	UNDERCARRIAGE LEG ASSY.	L98680A	G.A. OF VACUUM SYSTEM	98692A	ASSY. OF PIPES IN FUSELAGE
C98600A	FUSELAGE COMPLETE	G985A	CHASSIS TOP STRUCTURE ASSY.	L981905·6A	G.A. OF ENGINE INSTALLATION	98730·1A	ASSY. OF PIPES IN LEADING EDGE
C98601·2A	FUSELAGE SHELL HALVES	G98173A	ARRANGEMENT OF UNDERCARRIAGE	L98221S·8A	G.A. OF ENGINE SIDE	980421·2	PRESSURE VENTING OF DROP TANKS
C98603·4A	FUSELAGE SHELL HALVES COMPLETE	G98174A	TWIN BRAKE WHEEL ASSY.	L985055·6A	G.A. OF FIREWALL	98875A	ASSY. OF BROWNING GUN PIPES
C98692A	G.A. OF NAVIGATORS ARMOUR	J985A	ARRANGEMENT OF FIN	(SEE BELOW)	G.A. OF POWER UNIT	98662A	ARRANGEMENT OF CANNON COCKING HOSES
C98853A	ASSY. OF NOSE	J986A	ARRANGEMENT OF RUDDER	98L240A	G.A. OF EXHAUST SYSTEM	98018A	G.A. OF OXYGEN SYSTEM
E98289·0A	ASSY. OF FLAP	J98750A	ARRANGEMENT OF TAILPLANE	98N240A	G.A. OF BOMB WIRING	980104A	ASSY. OF BLIND FLYING PANEL
E98311·12A	ASSY OF AILERON	J98970A	G.A. OF TAIL WHEEL	98N374A	WIRING DIAGRAM	981A	G.A. OF CABIN HEATING & VENTILLATION
E98440A	G.A. OF WING	J98101BA	G.A. OF ELEVATOR	98N375A	THEORETICAL WIRING DIAGRAM	98303A	G.A. OF GUN HEATING
E98442A	WING ARRANGEMENT GENERAL	K98260A	ASSY. OF CONTROL COLUMN	98N460A	G.A. OF RADIO INSTALLATION	985A	G.A. OF DINGHY INSTALLATION
E98449A	ASSY. OF TOP SKIN	K98506A	G.A. OF FLYING CONTROLS	98N687A	G.A. OF BONDING	98206A	INSTALLATION OF BROWNINGS
E98482A	WING BOMB INSTALLATION	L985A	G.A OF ENGINE CONTROLS ON SPAR	98PB1A	G.A. OF FUEL SYSTEM	98400A	G.A. OF COCKPIT EQUIPMENT
E98495A	G.A. OF CONDUITS IN WING	L987·8A	G.A. OF ENGINE MOUNTING STRUCTURE	98P87	ARRANG'T OF FUEL & VENTING (LONG RANGE)	98447A	INSTALLATION OF 20MM. CANNONS
98F180A	G.A. EXTERNAL WING TANKS	L9811A	G.A. AND RIGGING OF ENGINE CONTROLS	P98429A	ARRANGEMENT OF TANK & VENTING SYSTEM	981050A	G.A. OF DESERT EQUIPMENT
F98334A	FRONT SPAR MAIN PLANE	L98267·8A	TOP ENGINE COWLING PANEL	Q98150A	G.A. OF TAIL WHEEL JACK	Z98405	RIGGING DIAGRAM

This superbly detailed wartime fold-out colour cut-away of an FB. Mk. 40 (FB. VI), is to be found in the 'Descriptive Manual' above left. It shows most of the main (subcontracted) sub-assemblies that go to make the complete aircraft.

PREPARED BY THE DE·HAVILLAND AIRCRAFT PTY LTD SYDNEY N.S.W.

MOSQUITO MK.40

COMPILED & DRAWN BY R.W. BECKHOUSE

De Havilland UK was not just limited to wartime production of the Mosquito; it was involved in many more activities, including flying training, Hurricane, Spitfire and Merlin repair, Tiger Moth production, engine manufacture etc.

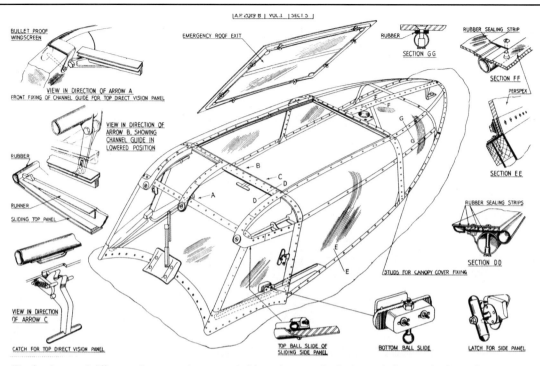

The fundamental difference between the two main Mosquito types lay in the cockpit canopies (apart from armament or lack of it). Above is the type found on the fighter/fighter-bomber/night-fighter/trainer and below the bomber/photo-reconnaissance type. (via David Wadman)

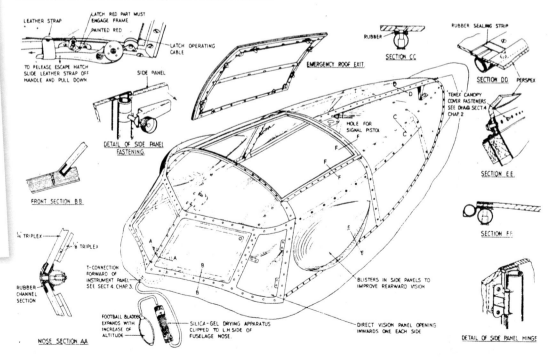

Typical armament for the F. II and FB. VI: 4 x .303 machine guns in the nose with 4 x 20 mm cannon in the lower fuselage belly.

The Mosquito FB. VI was a widely used mark, seeing use from 1943 through to post-war.
General Data for the FB. Mk. 40 (Australian FB. VI): Engines: Packard Rolls-Royce Merlin 31 or 33 (Merlin 21, 22, 23, 25 – UK built FB. VI). Performance varied widely depending upon role and equipment carried. Typical Max cruising speed: 365 mph at 20,000 feet. Max operating height: 33,000 ft. Fuel capacity: 713 Imp gal (2 x 50 gallon drop tanks and 63 gal long-range tank). Range: 1,855 miles. Wing Span: 54 feet 2 inches. Length: 41 ft 5 ins (tail up). Armament: 4 x 20 mm cannon, 4 x .303 in MG, 4 x 250 lb or 500 lb bombs (internally and externally), 8 x 25 lb or 60 lb rockets.

A fighter-bomber FB. VI Series ii. HX918 was a Hatfield-built example and was retained for a while by the A.A.E.E. for rocket projectile tests (seen here under the wing) in November 1943. This Mosquito eventually ended up with the Royal Norwegian Air Force on 15 August 1947 as SF-AR.

Two fundamental types were built: bomber and fighter-bomber. Visually the two differed primarily in their forward fuselage and canopy design. In the fighter (and bomber), the two-man crew sat side-by-side (the navigator sat on the right and slightly behind the pilot) behind a bulletproof, flat, one-piece (car-like) windscreen under a Perspex cockpit. The cockpit Perspex was attached to a thin internal, tubular, welded-metal frame, with the addition of a removable perspex panel in the roof for escape in an emergency. Entry to the cockpit was via a small door on the upper starboard side below the cockpit, which could also be jettisoned in an emergency. Armament consisted of four .303 machine guns in the extreme nose with four 20 mm cannon in the lower forward fuselage. The cannon were operated by a trigger and the machine guns by a press switch in the control column: a master switch was provided on the centre instrument stay. A camera gun in the nose operated when either the cannon or the .303 guns were fired.

The fighter-bomber could carry two 250 lb bombs in the rear of the cannon compartment (later models could take two 500 lb bombs) and one 250 lb bomb (or a 500 lb bomb) under each wing. Two wing drop tanks could be carried in place of the wing bombs or wing-mounted multiple rockets on rails in place of the bombs or drop tanks. Later developments allowed tiered rockets to be carried alongside drop tanks.

The unarmed bomber/PR, with a two-man crew, incorporated a more streamlined V-type windscreen split in two halves but with the same escape panel in the roof and general canopy structure. It had a Perspex nose-cone mounting an optically-flat downward-looking vision panel for the navigator/bomb-aimer to operate the bomb-sight or cameras in the PR version. Entry to the cockpit was via a trapdoor-like hatch much lower down on the starboard fuselage side with a second internal hatch that became part of the cockpit floor when closed.

The bomber carried a variety of loads. First production B. IVs carried 4 x 500 lb bombs. This increased to a single 4,000 lb 'cookie' bomb in later B. IV, B. IX conversions and production line B. XVIs. Some marks could also take 6 x 500 lb bombs, four internally with the other two on wing racks. The B. 35 was essentially post-war and carried the 4,000 lb bomb (peacetime RAF Mosquitoes rarely carried wartime operational weights such as wing-mounted ordinance). All bomber and PR types used a variety of drop tanks ranging in size from 50-, 100- and 200-gallon capacity.

Mosquito Aircraft Restorations, Auckland, New Zealand

Mosquito Aircraft Restorations was founded 18 years ago by Glyn Powell of Auckland, New Zealand. In order to build the aircraft it necessitated the remanufacturing of the fuselage moulds and jigs for the wings etc., which some thought an impossible task. Using modern Epoxy glue, which is superior to the wartime glues, the company can produce the main wooden components of either a bomber or fighter-bomber as originally produced by de Havilland's.
So far it has produced a bomber fuselage for the Mosquito Bomber Group in Windsor, Ontario and a fuselage, tailplane,

These could almost be rare wartime colour photographs of Mosquito production - but they are, in fact, fuselages and wings under construction in Auckland, New Zealand today, by Mosquito Aircraft Restorations. The company faithfully follows the original drawings and specifications of wartime manufacture, but using much improved Epoxy glue, which is stronger, has excellent waterproofing qualities and is better at preventing moisture ingress – a problem with wartime Mosquitoes. (Glyn Powell)

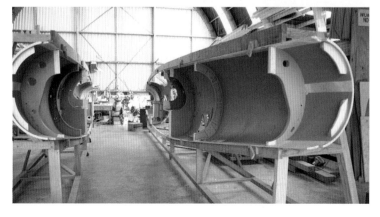

fin, wing and flaps for Gerald Yagen's Fighter Factory in Virginia, USA. This fighter-bomber is being restored to flight by Avspecs Limited in New Zealand (see opposite page) using components of FB. XXVI, KA114. At the time of writing, Glyn Powell owns the remains of an Australian-built T. Mk. 43, which he will restore to flight. He has started on this by working on the wing spars and ribs.
www.mosquitorestoration.com

AVSPECS Limited, Auckland, New Zealand

FB. XXVI, KA114, being rebuilt to flying condition by AVSPECS Limited of Auckland, New Zealand, for the Fighter Factory in Virginia, USA. It incorporates a new-build fuselage and flying surfaces by Mosquito Aircraft Restorations of Auckland, New Zealand. By the time this book goes to press, this Mosquito may very well have flown. (Warren Denholm - AVSPECS Limited, www.warbirdrestoration.co.nz)

Opposite page and right: The first photo-reconnaissance Mosquito PR 1, W4051, is seen here in its original camouflage (left) and in service with No. 1 PRU (right) now carrying the codes LY-U and early PRU colour scheme of dark slate grey and sky grey with PRU blue undersurfaces. Like all early PR and bomber Series i aircraft, it had short engine nacelles, early style exhaust design and short span tailplane. W4051 was the first Mosquito to join an RAF squadron – No. 1 PRU at Benson in Oxfordshire on 13 July 1941. It carried up to four cameras – one oblique and three vertical – with a variety of different combinations of cameras being used depending on the operation. Sometimes two of the vertical cameras were positioned together to form a single 'split' camera where two identical cameras would point at slightly different but overlapping areas. The resulting photos would provide stereoscopic coverage of the overlapping area as well as normal coverage of the extra areas. Amazingly this aircraft survived the war and was SOC on 22 June 1945. (Photographs opposite page top and far left BAE Systems, above right via Stephen Skinner)

AERIAL reconnaissance is an important factor in any war: being able to keep watch on an enemy, be it the movement of troops, munitions or monitoring industrial output, is crucial in determining how to plan and implement strategy and tactics to best counter the enemy. Britain embraced photo-reconnaissance enthusiastically in World War Two and developed it predominantly with the Spitfire and later, the Mosquito. Both aircraft had benefits. The Spitfire was, first and foremost, the best for short-range work, but the Mosquito had the benefit of twin-engine security and a much greater range. Both were to rely upon their speed, height and manoeuvrability in this role.

We will recall from Chapter Two that the agreement about using the aircraft for unarmed reconnaissance had saved the Mosquito. In early 1941 a revised contract conceded the need for 19 PR Mosquitoes plus a PR prototype: W4051. The first reconnaissance unit to receive Mosquitoes was No.1 Photographic Reconnaissance

Unit (No. 1 PRU) at Benson in Oxfordshire on 13 July 1941, when W4051 arrived to join the unit's Spitfires, with a further two production machines to follow by August. As mentioned earlier, the prototype W4050 had its fuselage replaced with the prototype PR. I fuselage destined for W4051 after the fuselage fracture at Boscombe Down on 24 February 1941. This enabled W4051 to be fitted with a production line PR fuselage, which subsequently saw it fly on operations, coded LY-U.

Squadron Leader Clarke of No. 1 PRU flew the very first operational sortie by any Mosquito on 17 September 1941 using W4055. This was a reconnaissance to the West Franco-Spanish Frontier. Unfortunately it proved unsuccessful owing to technical trouble which prevented the cameras from working, although Clarke was able to evade two Bf 109s. A sortie two days later proved to be more successful for W4055, when it made a successful flight to the Sylt-Heligoland area, with Flt. Lt. Taylor as pilot and Sgt. Horsfall as navigator. W4055 was to partake in 14 sorties before failing to return on her 15th operation over Bergen – the first Mosquito to be lost on operations.

PR Mosquitoes were quickly perceived to have high value in their intelligence role, due to their operational ceiling and high speed, and were soon ranging far and wide over Europe. The prototype W4051 scored a major coup on 22 February 1942 when, flown by F/L Ricketts on a trip to Kiel, she was able to photograph the battleship *Gneisenau* in dry dock undergoing repairs following the German's infamous 'Channel Dash'.

It is worth noting the mix of PR. Is and PR. IVs that were being used in these early operations, the PR. IVs being converted bombers. The aircraft's performance over the contemporary Bf 109 fighter had shown to be very good, but the gap was closing with improved versions of the Messerschmitt and the new Fw 190 introduced in the autumn of 1941. With the introduction into the PR. VIII of the two-stage Merlin in early 1943, it was found that the Mosquito regained the edge that the aircraft had had over enemy fighters under favourable conditions. On 3 March 1943 a PR. VIII from No. 540 Squadron became the first Mosquito to photograph the German capital of Berlin. The PR. VIII was essentially a PR. IV retrofitted with two-stage supercharged Merlin 61s as a quick performance fix

before the purpose-built PR. IXs came off the assembly lines. This 'quick fix' parallels the development of the Mk. IX Spitfire – which was essentially a Mk. V airframe with the Merlin 61, to help combat the new Fw 190.

The PR. IX was introduced in May 1943 with two-stage supercharged Merlin 72s, flown by No. 540 Squadron and 544 Squadron, introducing night photography into its role. On 12 October a 544 Squadron PR. IX, LR417, flown by F/L Merifield undertook the longest PR flight to date, flying to Trier, Regensburg, Linz, Vienna, Budapest, then back to Vienna, Sarbono, Bucharest, Foggia and Catania – a distance of over 1,900 miles in six and a half hours at 30,000 feet. LR417's engines quit as she taxied into the

In her element – PR. XVI, NS502 of 544 Squadron based at Benson, in PR blue and invasion stripes. It was later transferred to the Royal Navy, one of 24 and was SOC on 7 November 1947. Note the rear-view blister over the navigators position – allowing him to have a better view to the rear to warn the pilot of approaching Luftwaffe fighters. (via David Vincent)

An aerial photograph taken on 23 June 1943, by a PR Mosquito of 540 Squadron flown by F/S E. P. H. Peek of a test stand at Peenemünde showing V2s (A and B) on trailers. These were some of the first photos that reached the Allies showing the development the Germans were putting into this weapon.

Right: A V2 or Vergeltungswaffe 2, (reprisal weapon 2) also known as the Aggregat 4 (A4), which was developed at Peenemünde. The campaign against England opened on 8 September 1944 – with London's first strike, in Chiswick. (Artwork by Janusz Swiatlon)

PR Mosquitoes also saw service in the Far East where they flew some very long flights over sparsely populated jungle-covered regions under the control of the Japanese. This PR. XVI, NS524, of 684 Squadron, a Hatfield- built machine, was photographed in India. It was lost on 18 April 1945, when it crashed in bad weather near Dacca. (via Stephen Skinner)

gain in altitude, although its introduction into service was hampered by issues in the cockpit – misting of the perspex, lack of cabin heating and the need to fit cockpit blisters.

In the lead-up to the Allied invasion of France on 6 June 1944 and afterwards, PR

dispersal area. She had used her entire load of 760 gallons of fuel.

Some of the most invaluable work to be undertaken by PR Mosquitoes was the photography of the German V2 rocket development on the Baltic coast at Peenemünde by 540 Squadron on 22 April and later on 2, 12 and 23 June 1943. Such photography showed Allied intelligence the growing importance to the Germans of Peenemünde, which resulted in Bomber Command sending a large main force to bomb the research and development site in August (Operation *Hydra*). A short while later, intelligence suggested that a second, smaller pilotless aircraft, to be known as the V1, was also under development by the Germans at Zempin near Peenemünde. PR Mosquitoes and Spitfires ranged over much of northern France photographing numerous ski-jump like structures, all pointing towards London: these operations became part of '*Crossbow*', representing a joint British/American initiative against all phases of the German long-range weapons programme.

Developments in German Flak defences and the strengthening of the *Luftwaffe's* home-based fighter units showed the need for still higher speed and a higher ceiling. The PR. XVI was developed in late 1943, which was essentially a Mk. IX but with a pressure cabin and Merlin 76/77 engines and paddle blade propellers. It gave a useful

squadrons were at full strength, photographing a multitude of targets, which proved invaluable when it came to assessing the movements of the German armed forces. Never had aerial photography proved so important and the Mosquito played a key role at this most crucial time. This involved both day and night photography, using improved photo flash-bombs developed from the US for the night role. These M.46 flash-bombs generated 700,000,000 candle-power in one-tenth of a second. The use of photo-electric cells ensured that the target area photograph was taken at the peak of the flash.

The superiority of the Mosquito at height and speed was really put to the test with the *Luftwaffe's* introduction of its rocket and jet-powered interceptors in mid-1944. This was the first time that the *Luftwaffe* had any reliable means of intercepting the high-flying PR Mosquitoes (and PR Spitfires) – an inverse accolade if there ever was one. Typical of these encounters was the one on 15 August, when a Mosquito PR. XVI of No. 60 Squadron, South African Air Force, flown by Capt Saloman Pienaar and Lt Archie Lockhart-Ross, took off from San Severo in Italy to photograph Leipheim airfield in Germany. After flying up the Adriatic coast toward Prague, they turned to approach Munich from the northeast. As Pienaar recalled:

'I wasn't due to fly at all that day. Intelligence had called for a quick urgent flight over the Black Forest area. Normally you would never volunteer for another man's flight; it was considered very unlucky. But the pilot due to fly

SECRET   Report No. 2256

REPORTED INTERCEPTION OF P.R.U. MOSQUITO BY Me 262

It had been expected that the Me 262 would become operational in the near future, but the following is the first account of an interception by an aircraft answering the description of the Me 262. The crew of the Mosquito concerned have been interviewed by a Technical Intelligence officer, and a clear picture of the engagement obtained.

The Mosquito was on a photo-recce. flight, circling Munich for oblique shots, at a height of 30,000 ft. The aircraft was banking to port when the E/A was first observed, 400 yards astern and also banked to port. Subsequent events can be divided into 7 phases:

(1) Mosquito opened up to full boost and revs., attaining a speed of 200 A.S.I., (Approx.327 m.p.h. T.A.S.) which was increased to 260 A.S.I. by diving to 28,000 ft. E/A. also dived but (Approx. 412 m.p.h. T.A.S.) The pilot appeared 500 ft. above Mosquito, without having attacked. The pilot of the E/A when above the Mosquito banked sharply, apparently in order to scrutinise his quarry, and then turned away to port.

(2) E/A next appeared dead astern of Mosquito 1,500 to 2,000 yards away, quickly closing to 1,000 yards. The speed of Mosquito was 260 A.S.I. at 28,000 ft. (Approx. 412 m.p.h. T.A.S.). Mosquito started slight turn to port, but realised that E/A would be able to come out of the turn, so straightened up again. E/A opened fire at 800 yards. No apparent strikes.

(3) Mosquito turned to port, gradually steepening turn at 240 A.S.I., E/A (Approx. 380 m.p.h. T.A.S.) nose slightly up, to gain height. E/A appeared and followed in the turn, but Mosquito was always inside E/A's turning circle. E/A broke away to north; Mosquito turned south.

(4) After turning in wide circle, E/A again appeared on Mosquito's tail at 31,000 ft. Opened fire at 800 yards. No apparent strikes. Mosquito started to turn to port, tightening rapidly. E/A followed round, but after complete turn, was unable to get inside turn of Mosquito. E/A broke off first, in opposite direction to that of Mosquito.

(5) After wide turn, E/A appeared dead astern again, opening fire at 800 yards. No apparent strikes. Mosquito turned to port and tightened turn. E/A tried to follow round. Three complete turns were made in this manner, the Mosquito being always inside the E/A's turning circle. In fact, after the third turn, the Mosquito was on the tail of the E/A, and in a favourable position for attack had he been armed. Both aircraft were losing height. Mosquito broke off south towards mountains and cloud. E/A broke off to north.

(6) E/A repeated manoeuvre of a wide turn to north, coming round again on Mosquito's tail, but in a shallow dive, and disappeared under tailplane. Mosquito turned sharply to port at 240 A.S.I.,(Approx. 373 m.p.h. T.A.S.), stick hard back. Whilst in the turn two dull thuds were heard underneath Mosquito. E/A not in sight.

(7) Mosquito continued heading south for mountains and cloud cover, using full boost and revs. E/A next seen. Over mountains at 27,000 ft. E/A next seen 3,000 yards astern. Mosquito went into a dive, and weaved. Reached cloud cover. E/A overhauled, but comparatively slowly. E/A was 800 yards astern at 15,000 ft. On emerging from cloud, E/A made for another long bank of but did not open fire. Mosquito made for another long bank of clouds, and the E/A had closed to 450 yards by the time cover was reached. In cloud 3 to 4 minutes at 14,000 ft. On emerging, the E/A had disappeared. Mosquito climbed to 24,000 ft. and eventually saw Venice 30 miles ahead. Landed at Fermo.

After the two dull thuds were heard, the navigator attempted to open the emergency exit in preparation for baling out, if necessary.
/Great

-3-

3. It had a larger turning circle than the Mosquito, but this was in some instances outweighed by its superior speed.

4. The E/A invariably used a shallower dive than the Mosquito.

5. Most, if not all, attacks were delivered from the rear.

The pilot of the E/A may not have been sure of the identity of the Mosquito, and this may explain why he did not open his attack in the first instance, when he was in a favourable position to do so.

The pilot of the Mosquito turned south each time he broke away, believing, quite rightly, that the E/A had a fairly short endurance, and that by this means he could entice the E/A away from his supposed base.

At times it appeared that the high speed of the E/A was a disadvantage in that it rapidly overshot when coming up from astern, and had to make a wide turn in order to retrieve its position. The fact that it could make a wide turn, travelling in the opposite direction to that of the Mosquito to do so and still get into position again gives some idea of its superior speed.

It is interesting to note that the Mosquito used full boost and revs. for approximately 20 minutes, and that only a set of plugs was changed for the flight back to this country.

A.I.2(g)
D. of I.(R)
29th July,1944.

C.E.F. PROCTOR.
Wing Commander.

DISTRIBUTION

AIR MINISTRY		S.H.A.E.F.	
A.C.A.S.(I)	1	G - 2 Air Intelligence Sub-Division	1
A.C.A.S. (T.R.)	1		
A.C.A.S. (Ops.)	1	HOME COMMANDS	
D. of I.(O)		H.Q., A.D.G.B.	8
D. of I.(R)	1	H.Q., A.E.A.F.	5
D.D.I.2,	1	H.Q., 2nd T.A.F.	
D.O.R.		Air Tech. Int - W/Cdr. Wheeler	4
D. O. Ops.	1	Bomber Command	15
D. of Ops. (A.D.)	1	Coastal Command	19
D.B. Ops.	1	Transport Command	10
D.A.T.	1	H.Q., 100 (S.D.) Group	1
D. of Ops. (Tac.)	1		
R.A.F. Stn. Medmenham	2		
J.P.R.C.	2		
O.R.(P)	1		
C. Ops.3	2		
A.I.3.(U.S.A.)	16 + 2		
Air Tech. Sect.			
ASO-USSTAF	32		
U.S.N. Liaison Officer- A.I.2(g)	4		

Left: An Intelligence report on the first Me 262 attack on a PRU Mosquito, dated 29 July 1944. Unfortunately the second page of the report was missing.

Cockpit of an Me 262. Luftwaffe pilot Oblt. Kurt Welter of 10./NJG 11 is reported to have achieved 20 Mosquito victories by night and two by day – although some sources state up to 33 Mosquitoes were claimed. His claims have been the subject of much speculation and debate with official RAF losses stating about half this number lost. Nevertheless the Me 262 proved a real threat to Mosquito operations over the Continent by day and night during the latter half of the war. (US Army Signal Corps)

A SAAF 60 Squadron PR. XVI, possibly NS684 at San Severo, Italy, 1944. (via David Wadman)

'This wasn't a normal fighter at all...'

'He was a smart flyer...'

that day had a rotten cold and the other who might have stood in for him was at the end of his tour, so we were keeping him for the milk runs, which was the squadron tradition. We were at 30,000 ft. A nice afternoon it was too — warm with a little broken cloud as we headed up the Adriatic towards Prague.

'We turned off north-north-east of Munich and flew over an airfield named Memmingen, but I wasn't feeling very happy at all; it was too quiet, no Flak, no enemy fighters. We knew the enemy fighters well and they were no match for the Mossie, but the word was that this new fighter that they had was something else again.

'Archie was over the bomb-sight directing things for the six-inch and 12-inch mapping cameras, but we were also carrying the big 36-inch camera, which is for detail, and with that camera in operation you have to fly dead straight and level, otherwise you blur the photographs.

'At the next airfield, just a strip in fact, and very well camouflaged, Archie shouted: "I can see it ... There's a fighter taking off at a helluva speed!" I asked Archie to keep an eye on it because I was going nice and straight and level, but a few minutes later I picked up a speck in my rear-vision mirrors, directly behind the tail, but just a speck.

'Up to that time nothing could get at the Mossies, but this fighter must have climbed at well over 5,000 ft per minute, so I didn't dismiss this from my mind at all, especially when Archie said: "That's the fighter!"

'I took my eyes off that speck for only a few seconds, but when I glanced again there he was right on my tail, climbing into the attack and it didn't look like a normal aeroplane — that's for sure. This wasn't a normal fighter at all.

'So instead of turning left, I took the throttles, pitch levers and at the same time I hit the drop tank button and then I turned it to starboard. Just as I did so he fired and he hit the left aileron and blew it away completely. I was still in the turn to the right when this lot came off. I could see it out of the corner of my eye, but I didn't want to look too closely. Suddenly the aeroplane flicked left — it was losing all that lift on the left aileron, and the next moment I was in a spiral. In a spiral normally, the first thing to do is to roll it and get the power off, and I had the throttles right back, but it didn't make any difference; the boost was way up there and I could hear the engines screaming, but the plane was still going. I had full right rudder and when I pushed the stick forward, it just made a little ripple ... that's all.

'I can see it ... There's a fighter taking off at a helluva speed!...'

'It was down, down and when I heard the high blowers cut out I knew I must have been down to 19,000 ft. Then I saw the two throttles way back and the two pitch levers way up forward, so I pulled back the starboard engine pitch lever, and as I did so I could hear the revs come down and the plane just came back. So I was flying it with the stick right over to the right, right rudder full on and the left engine screaming its head off and boiling. The right engine revs had fallen, but the boost was still way up at the top.

'I was still trying to get things straight when Archie shouted: "Look out, here he comes again!" So all I did was to let go of everything and the aeroplane just flicked, to the left this time, and I saw him go past. I could see the Me 262 pilot was looking back at us ... He was a smart flyer and every time he made a pass he pulled up into the sun. He really was playing around with us with his enormous speed, but Archie was a wonderful fellow in these moments. He kept calling out when the Me 262 was a thousand yards away... firing range... but every time I turned to stay inside him I had to lose a bit of height.

'The third really concentrated attack was made when I was down to seven or eight thousand feet, but I was already making a little progress towards Switzerland and there was some low cloud, so I dived into it. But I realised that each time I evaded I had to lose some altitude, so that as he made his third run in, I said to Archie: "Well, here goes..." and I flipped the aircraft round and headed straight for the Me 262. After all, if we had to go, we

'...there was some low cloud, so I dived into it ...'

might as well have taken him with us! I saw him go straight over me ... I could just see his belly ... Then I dived into low cloud again. This was somewhere near Lake Constance. The head-on gave me a little more time, because the Me 262 had quite a wide radius of turn, but when I got into the clouds and looked at the artificial horizon it was perpendicular.

'*The final attack came at 500 ft, but I think by then this chap was running short of fuel and I just saw him go over me and break off. It was just as well because I couldn't fly the Mossie above 500 ft or the left engine would boil. The throttle was jammed full on and the linkage was damaged by that shell in the main spar. The right engine was still at full boost, but we reduced revs and that's the way we made it out, just skimming the hills and then losing altitude.*'

Eventually the crippled Mosquito managed to land back at San Severo where both crew members were awarded the DFC. Although the aircraft was written off, the mission did achieve one conspicuous success as its cameras managed to record some clear views of the Me 262.

Above: Lt Archie Lockhart-Ross and Capt Saloman Pienaar inspecting the damage to their PR. XVI, NS520 at San Severo after their encounter with an Me 262 near Munich on 15 August 1944. The impact of the Messerschmitt's cannon shells is very evident on the inboard flaps. Note also the missing rear fairing to the undercarriage nacelle. The circular recessed hole in the fuselage to the right of Pienaar is the ground starter socket hatch (the hatch itself is missing).

Major Daryl W. Allam, of Pretoria (centre), commander of No. 60 Squadron SAAF, is seen here congratulating Capt Saloman Pienaar (left) in front of NS520 after his encounter with the persistant Me 262 near Munich. At right is Capt E. R. Larter AFC, the other squadron flight-commander. (via Robert Forsyth)

The Mosquito PR. XVI was a widely used mark, seeing use from 1943 through to post-war.
General Data for the PR. XVI:
Engines: Rolls-Royce Merlin 72/73 or 76/77 two-stage supercharged.
Max cruising speed: 378 mph at 30,000 feet. Max speed: 415 mph at 28,000 ft. Max operating height: 36,000 feet. Max fuel capacity: 860 Imp gallons. Range: 2,400 miles. Max weight: 23,350 lb.
Wing Span: 54 ft 2 ins. Length: 41 ft (tail up). Cameras: K17 (6 inch), K17 (12 inch), F24 (5 inch), F24 (14 inch), F52 (36 inch), F52 (20 inch).

The Americans were supplied with 107 PR XVIs under Reverse Lend-Lease. They loved the aircraft and considered them 'hot ships', though like all, they had to come to terms with the swing on take-off (or landing) if not corrected – they coined the term 'a hollowed out log with a built in swing'! Mosquito PR. XVI, MM345, of the 653 Bomb Sq (L) (Wea Rcn) 25th Bomb Group, at left, was one of the first machines to be equipped with equipment capable of dropping 'Window' (strips of metallic foil used to confuse German radar) ahead of the lead bombers – these were known as 'Graypea' missions. They also would arrive over the target some 20 minutes ahead of the bombers reporting weather conditions, cloud level and enemy fighter activity. If the primary target was abandoned because of weather conditions they would move to the second or third target and begin again. As the bombers came in they would move out of the target area returning later to photograph the results. Their tails were painted red, 'Redtails' in an attempt to try to avoid US escort fighters from mistaking them for a twin-engine Luftwaffe aircraft. Other uses for the Mosquito were meteorological flights, known as 'Bluestockings'. These flights gathered weather information over the Continent to aid in the planning of bombing missions and, in addition, there were other operations called 'Skywave' – long-range navigation missions using LORAN. The PR. XVI MM388 bottom left was flown by the 654th Sq. (Special Rcn) 25th Bomb Group. This unit flew OSS (Office of Strategic Services) 'Joan-Eleanor' flights (later under the control of the 801st/492nd BG). This involved dropping trained OSS agents into occupied Europe who maintained contact in the field by carrying the portable 'Joan' radio with the 'Eleanor' transmitter/receiver set on the Mosquito operated by a third crewman in the rear fuselage. The transmissions operated on 260 MHz VHF band and remained virtually undetectable by the Germans and enabled the Mosquitoes to fly high and make contact with the agents. The agent made his report in plain speech, and the aircraft recorded the transmission on a wire recorder. Additionally, the aircraft could ask for immediate clarification if required, without the delay of encryption and decryption, or an intelligence officer aboard the circling aircraft could talk directly with the agent. The 654th flew at least 62 'Joan-Eleanor' flights and the 492nd BG 17 flights. In addition the Americans used the Mosquitoes for traditional PR work, both day and night. The night photography flights were known as 'Joker' missions and used 700-million M-46 cp photo flash bombs to light the area being photographed.

The PR Mosquito was to achieve its zenith in the European theatre with the introduction of the PR. 32, which was based on the PR. XVI. It had two-stage 113/114 Merlins, a pressure cabin and notably a lengthened and lightened wing to increase ceiling. This remarkable machine was introduced in late 1944 and could achieve 42,500 feet with a useful gain in speed, although as with its Mk. IX and Mk. XVI sisters, the German jet and rocket fighters were still to make operations a testing time indeed. One such encounter was with a PR. XVI, NS639 (see profile below), flown by F/L Dodd and F/S Hill of 544 Squadron on 16 September, when their aircraft was suddenly jumped by two Me 262s during a flight to Magdeburg. The two Messerschmitts made eight determined attacks on the Mosquito before it took safety in cloud at 6,000 ft.

PR Mosquitoes were introduced to the Far East in 1943, flying out of Calcutta, emulating their European cousins with their intelligence successes through the lens. These operating conditions tested man and machine and many notable flights were undertaken, often between five and eight hours in duration, some of the longest

Mosquitoes including the PR marks could carry a range of auxiliary fuel tanks under the wings, of 50-, 100-, and 200-gallon capacity.

Mosquito PR. XVI, NS639, G-AOCI, Thruxton, Hampshire, 1958

Typical of the varied lives many Mosquitoes were to have is NS639. She was
to survive her wartime RAF encounters with Me 262s over Germany with
544 Squadron (see text above) to see further use in the Royal Navy, post-war, as one of 24 PR. XVIs supplied. After her stint in the RN
she was sold in 1956 along with five other ex-RN PR. XVIs to a Mr R. A. Short who had them flown from the Royal Navy Air Station
at Lossiemouth into Thruxton aerodrome near Andover in Hampshire. NS639, with her RN colours whitewashed over, became
G-AOCI. She was fated never to leave Thruxton, unlike three of her sisters who went to the Israeli Air Force. In time the temporary
white-wash faded, revealing the old RN colours to clash with her civil registration (as seen here). The remaining Mosquitoes became
local landmarks on the airfield, slowly succumbing to weather and vandals. With engines and undercarriages removed, NS639
and the other remaining two were unceremoniously burnt in 1960.

The superlative PR. 32: even the large 100-gallon wing tanks, cannot hide the lines of this thoroughbred. Introduced into the European Theatre in late 1944, this improved PR. XVI incorporated a lengthened wing for increased ceiling with later type Merlin 113/114s and a pressure cabin. NS589 was a Hatfield-built machine and was the first PR. 32 (one of five) to see operational service, in this case with No. 540 Squadron on 5 December 1944. It completed 14 operational flights over Germany, principally photographing the rail network.

Below: This ex-RN PR. XVI, RG173, like G-AOCI (NS639) on page 44 (opposite), was another of the six Mosquitoes purchased by a Mr Short in 1956 and flown into Thruxton aerodrome. Registered G-AOCL, she too was destined never to leave Thruxton. Seen here in 1958, the Mosquito has already surrendered one of her Merlin engines to keep another flying. In October 1960, along with G-AOCI (NS639) and G-AOCK (NS753), she was burnt. During her time with the Royal Navy she had been fitted with four-bladed propellers. (Brian Doherty)

Above: The final development of the PR Mosquito was the PR. 34. A specially lightened airframe gave an increased ceiling of 3,000 feet. It did not see wartime service in Europe, principally seeing service in the Far East against the Japanese and later against the Communist terrorists in the Malayan Emergency in the 1950s. This example is a Royal Navy PR.34 photographed post-war at Gibraltar. PF664 was a Percival-built machine and was scrapped in 1958.

A fine photograph of PR 34, VL619 at Hatfield where she was built. Note the 200-gallon drop tanks which gave the aircraft a range of 2,500 miles. It carried two F.52 vertical cameras forward of the belly tank and one F.24 oblique camera aft of this tank plus two additional cameras in the aft fuselage. This Mosquito served with No. 13 Squadron at Fayid in Egypt and was SOC in September 1951. It was photo-reconnaissance in which the Mosquito first saw action in 1941 and 14 years later in December 1955, it was a PR. 34 Mosquito which undertook the last operational flight by a Mosquito in the RAF.

Below right: Central to any pilot familiarising himself with the Mosquito were the 'Pilot's Notes'. These original sets belonged to a F/L Cramer, who was very studious with any new official amendments in the handling notes – the copies here cover Mosquito Marks VIII, IX, XVI, PR 34 and B 35. All are littered with carefully pasted-in updates and signatures/dates for when the amendments were incorporated. F/L Cramer was to serve with 58 Squadron, which operated post-war with a mixture of PR 34s and Avro Anson C19s. (via John Howell)

Mosquito flights of the war. One particular PR. IX, LR464 of 684 Squadron, was flown out to India in December 1943 and flew its first operation in early January 1944. By the cessation of its operational career in late March 1945 it had flown some 90,000 miles over Japanese-held territories in 57 sorties, logging 495 flying hours, 320 of these on operations. Only once did it abort an operation due to a technical issue – a notable achievement indeed. RAAF PR Mosquitoes also operated from Australia's north on very long-range flights over Japanese-held territories – using a mix of PR. Mk. 40s and UK supplied PR. XVIs.

The final variant – not to see wartime use in Europe – was the PR. 34. This was a very long-range development with increased fuel load and removal of all armour and self-sealing from the fuel tanks to

Australia converted six FB. Mk. 40 Mosquitoes into unarmed PR. Mk. 40s to meet an urgent need within the RAAF for home-based photo-reconnaissance as procurement of US and British aircraft had proved difficult earlier in the war. The RAAF did operate a few P-38 Lightnings, but in the end they proved unsuitable.The PR. Mk. 40 operated with No. 87 (PR) Squadron (originally No. 1 PRU RAAF) founded in June 1942. At (right and far right) is the first Mosquito converted, A52-2, which became 87 Squadron's first Mosquito. In place of the nose-mounted machine guns were two F24 split vertical cameras with a third, an F52, mounted to the rear of the bomb bay (this camera arrangement was to change in later conversions with one K17 in the nose and two K17s or F24s in the rear fuselage). The operational base was at Coomalie Creek in the Northern Territory and it was from here that A52-2 made 38 operational flights, starting on 1 June 1944. She became known as 'Old Faithful'. These very long and hazardous flights were conducted over vast areas of the Dutch East Indies, the Celebes, Halmaheras and the Philippines – principally searching for Japanese airfields at this stage, but meteorological flights and Japanese naval shipping movements were also covered. By March 1945 PR. XVIs were arriving on strength from the UK and beginning operations – 23 served with the squadron. At right is PR. XVI, A52-609 ex NS726, taxiing out for the squadron's last wartime operation on 15 August 1945. This Mosquito was known as "Bosko's Bus" and carried out seven wartime operations. Note the propeller tip vortices, caused by the hot and humid conditions in the Northern Territory. (via David Vincent)

give a useful height increase of 3,000 feet. These high-flyers were introduced in June 1945 in the Far East, again with 684 Squadron, flying from the Cocos Islands on very long-range missions, the longest flight being 2,600 miles and taking just over 9 hours.

It is to be remembered that the PR Mosquito was the first of the type to see operational service with the RAF and it fell to a PR Mosquito to see it out of operational service. On 15 December 1955, RG314, a PR. 34, flew the last Mosquito operation in the RAF,

flown by F/O 'Collie' Knox and his navigator F/O J. Thompson. This Mosquito, and its sister aircraft and Spitfires of No. 81 Squadron, had been gathering photographic intelligence in the drive to expel Communist terrorists during the Malayan Emergency. For seven years from 1949 to 1955 these Mosquitoes had been operating in the Far East in an environment initially not suited to longevity for the airframes. The fact that they operated successfully for so long is testament to the soundness of the original design.

As related on the previous page, No. 87 (PR) Squadron's last wartime operational flight was on 15 August 1945. PR. XVI, A52-609 is shown beating up the airfield at Coomalie Creek in honour of this moment, (above, and below) with a prop feathered for the show. The smoke on the edge of the airfield below is a bush fire, an ever present aspect of the 'top end' country, locally known as 'scrub' or 'bush'. This Mosquito was lost on 26 January 1946 at Balikpapan in Borneo when it swung on take-off. The squadron continued to operate until disbandment on 24 July 1946, when personnel and aircraft were transferred to the Survey Flight, later known as No 87 (Survey) Squadron in 1948 (in November 1949 it regained its wartime title, No. 87 (PR) Squadron). The PR XVIs were replaced in 1947 with Australian-made PR Mk. 41s (opposite page) with two-stage Merlin 69s and the squadron operated with these until the end of 1953 in the successful aerial photographic survey of Australia. (via David Vincent)

A52-609's flight crew for the squadron's last operational wartime flight was F/L Maitland (second from right) and F/O Reedy (third from right) seen here with the backbone of any squadron – the ground crew. (via David Vincent)

RAAF PR. Mk. 41, A52-314 started out as a FB. Mk. 40, A52-205 and like a number of these airframes (28 in all), it was later converted to a PR, gaining two-stage Merlin 69s, cameras and a new serial. This evocative photograph of A52-314 (above) was taken at Forest Hill RAAF base in NSW in 1958 (now RAAF Base Wagga) during an air show. It was in use as a 'gate guardian' and instructional airframe and still existed in 1966 before being burnt! The photograph at right shows it still relatively complete, apart from removal of its tyres, which has caused its undercarriage struts to sink into the ground. Behind her is a CAC Wirraway – the very last one to succumb to the scrap-man at Wagga. (Top photograph courtesy Ken Merrick)

Above: Purportedly, this photograph shows A52-314 being burnt in the 1960s at Wagga, but study of the roundels shows these to be of the earlier wartime RAAF style, which continued in use into the late 1940s. Whilst it does not appear to be A52-314, it shows the same fate that aircraft suffered.
(Above and left via Les Homer)

W4072 was an early Bomber B. IV Series i, with short nacelles and original exhaust cowling design. The paint scheme was the early style dark earth/dark green with A1 roundels with yellow borders, and the underside was sky blue. This Mosquito joined 105 Squadron and took part in the first Mosquito bomber operation on 31 May 1942 as a follow-up to the '1,000 bomber raid' the night before on Cologne. Coded as GB-D, it was flown by Sqn Ldr Oakeshott, carrying 4 x 500 lb bombs and departed at 0400 hrs. The second Mosquito, W4064, GB-C, crewed by Plt Offs Kennard and Johnson, left at 0630 hrs. W4064 was never seen again – the first Mosquito bomber to be lost on operations. It was hit by flak and crashlanded at Bazel in the Netherlands. W4072 eventually passed to No. 627 Squadron and was ditched off Essex, 9 January 1944, returning from a raid to Berlin.

UNARMED IN BATTLE 5

An early wartime illutration of a Mosquito bomber.

Far right: GB-E, DZ353, a B. IV Series ii of 105 Squadron. The Series ii was identifiable by its extended production nacelles and later style exhaust shroud design. GB-E was photographed in a series of well-known in-flight shots with another of the unit's Mosquitoes, DZ367. She was flown on this occasion (opposite) by Wg Cdr Roy Ralston and F/L Sid Clayton. DZ353 eventually passed to 627 Squadron and went missing on 9 June 1944. (via Michael Davies)

ALTHOUGH Bomber Command was a little sceptical about the Mosquito bomber, it nevertheless began its operational career in early 1942 with No. 105 Squadron, a part of No. 2 Bomber Group based at Horsham St. Faith. On 31 May 1942 this unit's Mosquito B. IVs had their baptism of fire with a daylight attack on Cologne as a follow-up to Bomber Command's first 1,000 bomber raid the night before. Four Mosquitoes were sent out at different times and one failed to return. Later that day, Sqn Ldr Channer left Horsham to make a general reconnaissance of the German city and upon arrival made a shallow dive at nearly 380 mph over some railway yards and fields where neither people nor livestock reacted until he was well past. This gave good cause in his mind to use the aircraft on selected targets where its speed and surprise capability could be used. It has to be remembered that the Mosquito was a new concept in bombing and much thought was being given as to how best to use it in these early days.

On 8 June 1942, 105 Squadron was to share its airfield – and initially even its aircraft – with Bomber Command's second Mosquito squadron to come into operation, No. 139 (Jamaica) Squadron. This squadron flew its first operation on 24/25 June when Sqn Ldr Houlston flew a low-level attack on an airfield near Wilhelmshaven just after dusk.

Initially, the B. IV came in Series i form followed by the Series ii guises. Around ten Series i's were built, identified by their short engine nacelles. But around 263 Series ii's were built with lengthened nacelles to cure tail-buffeting. This new nacelle design was to be seen on all subsequent Mosquitoes and both squadrons were to use a mixture of these two types.

The real test for these Mosquito bombers and the basis for de Havilland's design ethos was how it was going to cope with fighter opposition. This came to the fore on 2 July when three Mosquitoes from 105 Squadron and two from 139 Squadron attacked the submarine pens at Flensburg. Over the target they ran into Flak and a mixed force of Bf 109s and Fw 190s. Two Mosquitoes were lost to fighters, with one crew killed and the other becoming POWs, though the other Mosquitoes were able to use their superior speed at sea-level to evade the fighters. Was this vindication for the Mosquito's ability? Hard experience was to show that, if a pursuing fighter could be spotted in time, the Mosquito could keep it at a distance and employ the 'corkscrew' method of evasion but if the enemy fighter had height on its side to dive, so building up speed, it could be a very

This page: Fine views of 105 Squadron B. IVs Series ii at Marham, warming up and taxiing in 1942 and at rest with 139 Squadron waiting for the next operations (below left). Ever on the look out to squeeze extra speed out of the Mosquito bomber on these early operations, ground crews were persuaded to polish the aircraft; this could increase the speed by as much as 8 mph – a difference between life and death. A sobering thought given the aircraft's strengths is that virtually all of the 105 Squadron Mosquitoes on this page went missing on operations with the exception of one damaged in action – E-GB, DZ353 (as related on page 51), failed to return on 9 June 1944; J-GB, DZ367, failed to return on 30 January 1943; P-GB, DZ336 ?; K-GB, DZ378, damaged on 20 February 1943; H-GB, DZ379 (see also opposite page), failed to return on 18 August 1943 and A-GB, DZ360, failed to return on 22 December 1942.

105 Squadron ground crew load four 500 lb bombs into a Mosquito B. IV at Marham.

A fine study of a 105 Squadron B. IV, H-GB, DZ379 at Marham with bomb trolley in front, ready to take its allocated 4 x 500 lb bombs. By now Mosquitoes had changed their camouflage, as seen on page 50, to upper surfaces of dark green/ocean grey with under surfaces in medium sea grey, carrying type C1 roundels on the fuselage. Despite their speed, Mosquitoes didn't always have it their own way. These early operations, which were high-level daylight raids, were not without cost and, in time, increasing numbers of Mosquito bombers were being lost – a crew a week – with lower-than-average bombing results. This was to change in time with development of new tactics, resulting in the Mosquito bomber having one of the lowest loss rates by wars end. Though unfortunately this Mosquito went missing on 18 August 1943 when part of 139 Squadron on a raid to Berlin.

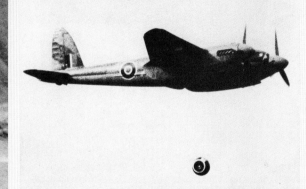

Left: DK290 was a B. IV used in experiments for the smaller version of the Barnes Wallis 'bouncing bomb' (based on 'Upkeep', which was used against German dams by 617 Squadron). Called 'Highball', the specially modified Mosquitoes were designed to carry two of these smaller weapons for use in anti-shipping operations. 618 Squadron was formed on 1 April 1943 to work up on the weapon (below left). In July 1944 news was received that the squadron was to move to the Pacific area for anti-shipping duties against the Japanese. The squadron arrived in Australia on 23 December 1944, but ultimately the weapon was never used in anger. The squadron was disbanded in Australia on or around 27 July 1945 and the unit's Mosquitoes based at RAAF Station Narromine in NSW remained stored in the open for some time until their fate could be decided. By mid 1947 it was decided to offer the aircraft as scrap where they stood. 14 of the aircraft were virtually complete including Merlin engines at £35 each! Another 22 were engineless for £22 each. Many went to local farmers and the curious. Note that DK290 (top) is shown here wearing day fighter colours, with a sky band and spinners, in a short-lived idea intended to give Luftwaffe fighters the false impression that they were Mosquito fighters.

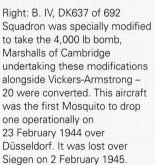

Right: B. IV, DK637 of 692 Squadron was specially modified to take the 4,000 lb bomb, Marshalls of Cambridge undertaking these modifications alongside Vickers-Armstrong – 20 were converted. This aircraft was the first Mosquito to drop one operationally on 23 February 1944 over Düsseldorf. It was lost over Siegen on 2 February 1945.

At right is the cockpit of a British-built B. IV and far right the cockpit of a Canadian-built B. IV, known as the B. XX in Canada. The principal difference lay in the cockpit instruments – the Canadian version used US-sourced instruments.

A wartime cartoon poking fun at (for some) the Mosquito's rather cramped cockpit and difficult accessibility.

"He says it's not his affair how we get in—and if we're not airborne in one and a half minutes we get no leave."

different story. One worthwhile development stemming from these early encounters was the adoption of a Perspex blister in the canopy roof, which enabled the navigator to kneel on his seat facing aft and give a better warning to the pilot over the RT about any fighters coming up behind. Crews on these daylight operations called the intercepting *Luftwaffe* fighters 'Snappers'. These early operations, which were high-level daylight raids, were not without cost and, in time, increasing numbers of Mosquito bombers were being lost – a crew a week – with lower-than-average bombing results. This did not, however, diminish the high morale in the Mosquito squadrons; they knew they had a winner. At an operational level, many knew how best to operate – go in at low level and at dusk.

In September 1942, two raids were to increase the Mosquito's

standing. The first was the inaugural daylight raid on Berlin on the 19th, although it was unsuccessful due to weather and the *Luftwaffe*. For this raid, six Mosquitoes from 105 Squadron took off at 1230 hours and with cloud obscuring the target made for Hamburg, which was also found to be obscured. During this operation the Mosquitoes suffered numerous attacks by fighters. The Combat Report for the operation makes chilling reading, '*DISPOSITION: 2 other (Mosquito) aircraft in close company, 1 ahead and 2,500' above on starboard bow, 1 level on starboard quarter. Tactics: 1 e/a believed Fw 190 approx 1,000 yards away on starboard beam level coming in to attack. Mosquito carried out diving turn to port into cloud 5000' below and evaded e/a. Mosquito a/c flying straight and level on starboard quarter was attacked from astern and 500' below by e/a believed Fw 190 which fired burst into Mosquito whilst climbing. Burst of black smoke from Mosquito's port engine which did a stall turn to port and last seen spiralling vertically downwards with e/a following. Lesson: It is essential that a close watch be maintained for e/a throughout flight particularly so after emerging from bank of cloud. The aircraft which was shot down had obviously not seen the e/a.*' The lost Mosquito was GB-M, DK326, flown by S/L Norman Messervy, DFC, an Australian from Perth, and his observer P/O Holland.

The second high-profile raid was the very first of the low-level pinpoint attacks that were to make the Mosquito so famous – in this case the assault on the *Sicherheitspolizei* or *Gestapo* (HQ) in the Foreign Ministry Building in Oslo on the 25th. This raid was inspired

captured the Norwegian public's imagination and reminded them that they had not been forgotten and, even under the gaze of the occupiers, they rejoiced in the streets and placed flowers in their hundreds on a lake south-west of Oslo where one of the Mosquitoes crashed after being shot down by an Fw 190 of JG 5. All surviving crews faced determined attacks by Fw 190s but made it back.

In time tactics were changed with high-level operations tailoring off in September 1942, with the emphasis on low-level strikes. A new technique was employed combining shallow dive attacks with high-speed passes in order to confuse anti-aircraft defences. A second wave soon after the first was intended to cause much confusion and enabled a quick low-level escape. Adding to this confusion was the dropping of delayed-action bombs.

105 and 139 Squadrons were to continue blazing a trail in operations, carving a niche within the story of Bomber Command. Although the Commander-in-Chief himself, Air Marshal Arthur Harris, showed little initial enthusiasm for the Mosquito in these early days, this was to change. His indifference was quite contrary to the mood the aircraft created at squadron level. One wonders what would have happened if Mosquitoes had been available in higher numbers

Left, above and below: Three superb views of B. IV, DZ313 up from Hatfield on a pre-delivery test-flight. The Mosquito became well known through this series of air-to-air photographs and for many people these were to be their first views of it. They appeared in many early wartime articles on the Mosquito, principally in 'Flight' and 'The Aeroplane' in December 1942 and January 1943 respectively. De Havilland used the photograph below left for a DH advertisement which appeared in 'Flight' on 18 February 1943. DZ313 went on to join 105 Squadron, code E-GB and sadly was lost by the time these photographs were released on 20 October 1942, on an operation to Hannover. F/S Laurence Deeth and observer, W/O Frank Hicks, were killed. These photographs were taken by John Yoxall for 'Flight' earlier in 1942. (Photo at left: FLIGHT International www.flightglobal.com)

by a plea from the Norwegian Resistance Movement. Four Mosquitoes from 105 Squadron took off from Leuchars and raced out across the North Sea. One of the pilots, Pete Rowland, recalls: '*What a beautiful little aircraft this is, I thought, looking to my right at the trim silhouette of the leading Mosquito, its carpentered lines, slender, its tail cockingly high, the Rolls-Royce engines gulping down the miles. It was camouflaged earth-brown and tree-green above, sky-blue below; on the fuselage stood out the letters GB, for 105 Squadron. The Mosquito, tough, belligerent, swashbuckling – fastest two-seater in the world…*'[1]

The Mosquitoes were to place their bombs with accuracy but most passed through the building. Nonetheless, the raid

Luftwaffe fighters were called 'Snappers' by Mosquito bomber crews on these early daylight raids into Europe and the new Focke-Wulf Fw 190 (above) exemplified this term very much. It carried a heavier armament than the Bf 109 and proved to be a formidable foe for the Mosquito B. IVs, where early detection and speed were the Mosquito crews only defence.

[1]. *Mosquito Thunder, No. 105 Squadron RAF at War 1942-45*, Stuart R. Scott, Sutton Publishing, Gloucestershire, 1999.

The B. IX was an improved version of the B. IV, powered by two-stage Merlin 72s, the first Mosquito bomber to be powered by these new Merlin engines which benefited the aircraft in speed and altitude. This aircraft, LR495, was used at the A.A.E.E. in 1943, in a series of overload trials to take into account proposed increases in bomb loads (note the 500 lb bombs under the wings). It was destroyed on take-off during these overload trials on 29 January 1944. (via David Vincent)

Probably the most successful Mosquito night bomber, credited with 213 sorties in all. Mosquito B. IX, 'F-Bar' for Freddie, LR503 first saw action with 109 Squadron on 28 May 1943, before passing to 105 Squadron on 10 March 1944, primarily operating with the Light Night Striking Force carrying Oboe, hence the painted-over nose perspex and additional whip aerial in the profile. The aircraft is shown below after its 203rd operation, when the slogan '203 & still going strong' was chalked on the nose. For this operation it had been crewed by F/L T. P. Lawrenson (Pilot) and F/L D. W. Allen, DFC (Navigator). Its last operational mission was to Leipzig on 10 April 1945.

Left: LR503 took part in the 8th Victory Loan Drive in Canada in early May 1945, flown over to Canada by F/L Maurice Briggs (Pilot) DSO, DFC, DFM and F/O John Baker, (Navigator) DFC and Bar. Unfortunately whilst undertaking a very low-level 'beat-up' at Calgary Airport on 10 May 1945, the Mosquito hit a steel anemometer tower and flag pole atop the control tower, which severed the port wing and tailplane. The crash that followed took the lives of a most valued and decorated crew. A minor note in the Mosquitoes short sojourn in Canada, was that it would appear that it was virtually repainted for the tour, including its bomb log – LR503 looking nothing like it did during its time with 105 Squadron.

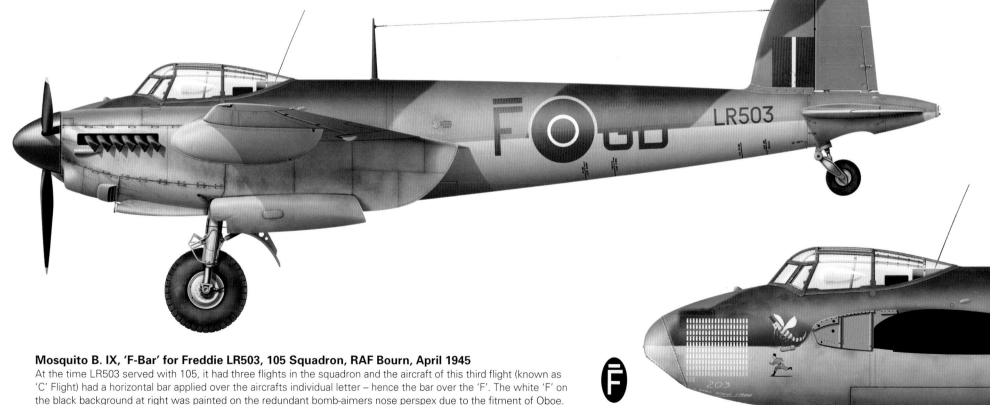

Mosquito B. IX, 'F-Bar' for Freddie LR503, 105 Squadron, RAF Bourn, April 1945
At the time LR503 served with 105, it had three flights in the squadron and the aircraft of this third flight (known as 'C' Flight) had a horizontal bar applied over the aircrafts individual letter – hence the bar over the 'F'. The white 'F' on the black background at right was painted on the redundant bomb-aimers nose perspex due to the fitment of Oboe.

A Mosquito that never returned to base. Probably from either 105 or 139 Squadron, after capture, this almost intact de Havilland Mosquito B. IV was delivered to the 2./Versuchsverband OKL, nicknamed the 'Zirkus Rosarius', for combat evaluation. It was displayed at the Rechlin test centre on 19 September 1943 together with many other captured Allied aircraft, and carried the unit code T9+XB. All the Allied aircraft tested by this unit were painted with yellow tails and underside surfaces, to make them easily identifiable by Luftwaffe pilots and their Flak units. At the time this photograph was taken the Mosquito was minus its propellers. Other photographs of the machine on display show a hastily fabricated undercarriage of steel tube, using the original tyres, and also crushed lower cowling carburettor intakes which indicate the aircraft made a heavy landing in enemy territory ripping off the propellers and the undercarriage. The fabled Mosquito seems to have attracted much interest and probably some head-scratching as to how the British could make such a beautiful, but equally effective weapon out of wood – perhaps the very thoughts of the gentleman in the foreground with his hands behind his back! As far as can be ascertained this was the only complete Mosquito to be sent to the 2./Versuchsverband OKL and it never flew. Note the Spitfire in the background, also minus its propeller.

at the beginning of the bombing campaign. Major Hereward de Havilland said in a letter to his brother: '*Air Marshal Harris told me that he had, quite frankly, been surprised at the success Mosquitoes had had on low-level attacks, and he said as much in a letter he addressed to the units concerned.*' However, 'Bomber' Harris still had his priorities. The letter continued: '*But he still considers that only a very small force should be diverted from the normal bombing routine for this type of work. For Pathfinding which, he stated, will become the most important of all duties, the Mosquito is indispensable.*'

Germans who tuned to their radio sets at 11.00am on 30 January 1943 to hear *Reichsmarschall* Hermann Göring, Commander-in-Chief of the *Luftwaffe,* speak at a large Nazi Party rally in Berlin heard their broadcast cut short due to the distinct sounds of bomb blasts in neighbouring districts of the city. The blasts were from three 105 Squadron Mosquitoes who had turned up to interrupt the speech in clear skies with no Flak or fighters! This was a clear success after their failure to reach the capital after the first attempt in September 1942, not to mention Göring's idle boast to Berliners '*That no enemy aircraft shall fly over the Reich…*' Another three Mosquitoes from 139 Squadron followed this up later in the day to interrupt Goebbels' speech at around 4.00pm, though by this time Flak and fighters were on the alert and one of the Mosquitoes was unfortunately lost. Whilst this operation was of little military value at the time, it was a great propaganda coup and actually gave planners, after studying the aircraft departure times, fuel consumptions and bomb loads, ideas for future Mosquito attacks on Berlin.

Early 1943 saw the introduction of the B. IX with two-stage Merlin 72s. This provided a notable improvement in speed and altitude performance which came just in time, as the demands upon the Mosquito were increasing due to the introduction of heavier bomb loads and electronic aids with corresponding increased take-off weights, not to mention improved versions of both the Bf 109 and Fw 190 that were being encountered. But the B. IV was still being used on operations, and having to contend with the *Luftwaffe* as the following account shows from a 139 Squadron B. IV, DZ418, XD-M on 3 March 1943. The squadron ORB states, '*This A/C took off to attack the Flotation Plant at the Molybdenum Mine, Knaben and on the return journey at position 58.23'N.06.15'E (approx) on a course of 245 degrees at 1442 hours height 50 ft. Two F.W.190's were sighted in line astern about 500 yards away to port. Mosquito went down into a valley to evade enemy A/C which followed down the valley the winding nature of which prevented them from getting into position to make attack until the Mosquito crossed the coast at Stapnes when own and enemy A/C dived down to sea level. Immediately on crossing coast one E/a made an attack from directly astern at a range of 200 yards severing Mosquito's starboard rudder control, both elevator trimming wires and air speed indicator tube, also damaging hydraulic pipes with the first burst as Mosquito was taking evasive action by turning to starboard. Several other attacks were made without success one E/a sitting on Mosquito's tail and the other standing away to starboard to prevent our a/c turning in that direction. Mosquito took evasive action by turning into attacks and making climbing and diving turns at near sea level as possible. The second attack was made from starboard and above, the remainder from astern. E/a finally broke away position 58.15'N 06'02'E. (approx) 1447 hrs. 50 ft, only for Mosquito to find two more F.W.190's sitting on his tail in line astern about 400 yards away when Mosquito was steering a course of 180 degrees. These E/a took up similar positions to the first one, one directly astern the other standing off to starboard, attacks being made from directly astern by first one E/a and then the other as they changed position. Fire was opened up at a range of 3/400 yards, and several attacks were made, Mosquito took evasive action once again by making climbing and diving turns and sustained no further hits. E/a/c eventually broke off the attack from about 50 miles out to sea. Air speed indicator became U/s after Mosquito was hit, but by time attacks were made by second two E/a/c air speed is estimated at 320.*'

1 June 1943 saw Bomber Command's 2 Group Mosquitoes relinquish their current roles and join No. 8 Bomber Group, known as the Pathfinder Force (PFF). The PFF was formed within Bomber Command in January 1943 as a means of marking targets accurately with flares or T.Is. (Target Indicators), thus allowing the heavies and bomber Mosquitoes to attack more precisely. The Mosquito was perfect for the role. 105 and 139 Squadrons joined the PFF alongside 109 Squadron, which was using a mixture of electronic navigational aids, notably *Oboe* and *Gee*, for both night and day operations. *Gee* picked up signals from radio beacons in Britain and gave the aircraft's position, using a form of triangulation. *Oboe* involved two radars set up in Britain, one named 'Cat' which tracked the Mosquito along a constant-range path, the other named 'Mouse' which determined when it was over the target, at which point bombs were released. The first time a Mosquito dropped bombs guided by *Oboe* was on 20/21 December 1942 by a 105 Squadron B. IV.

The Mosquito B. IX was well established by 1943, enabling the units to fly higher and faster for night-time 'ops', while still maintaining high bombing accuracy due to *Oboe*. Even at heights of 30,000 feet, accuracy was often within 100 yards of the aiming point. *Oboe* was almost as accurate as clear daylight bombing, though it had limitations due to range. Strategically, it put *Oboe* in range of the Ruhr Valley, Germany's industrial heartland, and PFF Mosquitoes fitted with *Oboe* embarked upon the 'Battle of the Ruhr' in March 1943, marking Essen for a raid by Bomber Command 'heavies'. *Oboe* was not without problems and yet often during squadron training, with crews working up on it, it would function perfectly. On operations however, it became a different matter with crews returning with a 'failure of the precision device' reference to *Oboe*, due to its secret nature. Nevertheless, the fitment of *Oboe* and *Gee* to Mosquitoes constituted a major leap in the usage of the aircraft. The Mosquito's reputation in this new role blossomed, which was not lost within higher command. Hereward de Havilland noted the low loss rate for sorties flown – 0.4 per cent (only three aircraft) for 750 night operations. He noted: '*It will be possible to attack any target within about 400 miles of the English coast with 4,000lb bombs by day and night, in any but the worst kind of weather, with considerable accuracy and low losses; if the repeater system is successful, targets 700 miles away will be within range, with a smaller bomb load. One feels, in view of the bombing accuracy now obtainable from high and low levels, the great confidence all crews have in the Mosquito, and its relative immunity from attack...*'

F/O Joe Patient and his navigator of 139 Squadron had a most eventful evening when sent to Berlin on the night of 16/17 September 1943 in B. IV, DZ355 along with four other Mosquitoes. The squadron Operation Record Book (ORB) comments: '*The main excitement, however, was experienced by F/O Patient. He was hit over the*

The C-in-C of Bomber Command Air Marshal Harris, who in the early period of the Mosquito's development was somewhat of a sceptic as to its success but who, in time, became a great supporter of it. This was especially the case in the Pathfinder role: his heavy bombers were able to bomb the Reich with greater accuracy due to the dropping of flares or T.Is. (Target Indicators) by Mosquitoes.

Alongside the *Oboe*-equipped units was the 'Light Night Striking Force' (LNSF), another new chapter in the growing versatility of the Mosquito. No. 139 Squadron was to become part of the LNSF force. These constituted Mosquitoes operating *Gee* and *H2S*, which was a ground-scanning radar system. *H2S* was designed to identify targets on the ground at night or in poor weather – true blind-bombing radar. Mosquitoes of the LNSF, equipped with these electronic aides conducted a range of sorties across Germany for the remainder of the war, causing much disruption to the enemy defence net in support and indirect support of the heavier bombers. Some of these operations, known as '*Spooks*' were nuisance raids designed to mislead the enemy into thinking the Main Force targets were where the Mosquitoes were operating, thus tying up resources, particularly the *Luftwaffe's* night-fighters. In time, those units conducting '*Spooks*' carried out bombing raids not as feints, but as targeted raids in their own right. Aluminium strips known as '*Window*' (or chaff) were often used on these nuisance raids, dropped in quantity from the Mosquitoes to jam German *Würzburg* radar, the control tool for Flak and night-fighters. *Window* constituted a strip of coarse black paper, 2 cm wide by 25 cm long, with one side made of aluminium metallic foil. Tests had shown that if dropped in quantity it could confuse or swamp these radar screens as well as the airborne *Liechtenstein* radar in the night-fighters, thus hopefully denying an interception. It was used for the first time on the opening raid of the 'Battle of Hamburg' on 24/25 July 1943.

One of the greatest changes to take place with Mosquito bomber operations was the introduction, in early 1944, of the 4,000 lb bomb ('Blockbuster' or 'Cookie' as they were known) in place of the conventional 4 x 500 lb bombload. The idea was first mooted in early 1943 with tests conducted on a modified B.IV and a B. IX. True, the B. IV could carry the increased weight, but at the cost of some instability and poor single-engine performance. With the

Left: Marshalls in Cambridge undertook much conversion work on Mosquitoes during the war and one contract was for the conversion of B.IV and some B.IX to take the 4,000 lb bomb. (Stephen Skinner)

Right: A 4,000 lb bomb, suitably emblazoned with 'Happy Xmas Adolf' is wheeled before 'Q for Queenie' a B. XVI of 128 Squadron of the Light Night Striking Force (LNSF) at Wyton, prior to a night-bombing mission. The crew were F/O McEwan DFC and F/O Harbottle DFC and Bar.

target and had to feather his starboard engine. On his long stooge home he was coned twice, and lost a lot of height each time. Over Holland he was attacked by two Fw 190s, which pumped a good deal of cannon and machine gun bullets into his wings and fuselage. Eventually he staggered at low level to Manston, where he made a good crash landing, five minutes after his petrol had registered zero. Just as he came to a stop, a Typhoon nipped up behind him and removed the whole of his tailplane. Both aircraft were written off. Fortunately nobody was hurt.'

Typical of the *Oboe* squadron operations were those in support of the Allied invasion of France on 6 June 1944, when 105 and 109 Squadrons sent 25 Mosquitoes to mark gun emplacements on the Normandy coast for the following heavy bombers. The next night they marked rail targets near Caen using T.Is. (Target Indicators) and marked further rail networks deeper into the surrounding area. On D-Day, led by marker aircraft from 139 Squadron, other Mosquitoes from 692 Squadron and 571 Squadron mounted an operation on railway marshalling yards at Osnabrück using 4,000 lb bombs in an attempt to stifle the flow of German war materials to the invasion front.

Above: Fresh Percival-built B. XVIs await flight-testing and ultimate dispatch to operational units. Note how far the camouflage has come down on to the cowlings - an unusual feature on a Mosquito. PF563 was damaged on 22 May 1945 at Woodbridge, PF561was converted to a TT. 39 (see page 66) and went to the Royal Navy on 18 December 1947 and PF564 was delivered 1944/45. Served at Woodbridge, ATEU and Bomb Ballistics Unit. Said to have been given MU serial 6997M in 1950, but seen with her original serial still in 1952.

Mosquito B. XVI, P3-A, MM183 of 692 Squadron at Graveley in 1944, awaits loading of its 4,000 lb bomb. This unit was part of the LNSF and was formed on 1 January 1944. MM183 belly-landed at Manston after an engine cut on 1 February 1945.

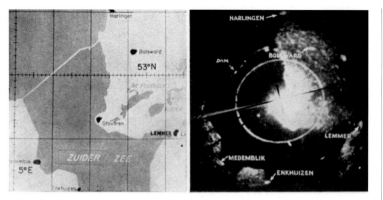

Far left: H2S equipment in the cockpit of a Mosquito bomber of 8 Group – PFF or Pathfinder Force. H2S was designed to identify targets on the ground at night or in poor weather – true blind-bombing radar. The two images at left show how it worked. The H2S image on the right is a scan of a dam across the Zuider Zee. This image would be seen in the cathode ray tube in the cockpit. The central part of the picture must be neglected, but outside of this the radical traces are clearly seen at their weakest where water reflects, or rather does not reflect; strong where land is below, and strongest when there are buildings.

introduction of the two-stage Merlin 72/73 and 76/77 in the B. IX and B. XVI in early 1944, here were aircraft that could 'happily' take the 4,000 lb bomb up to an operating height of 35,000 feet. The B. XVI was designed from the outset to take the 'Blockbuster' with earlier bomber variants to be modified accordingly. Marshalls in Cambridgeshire undertook some of these modifications, mainly to B. IV and a few B. IXs. Their swollen bomb bay doors identified these 'Cookie'-equipped Mosquitoes, giving the aircraft the appearance of being 'pregnant'. With this development, there was a return to more conventional Mosquito bomber squadrons, often being led to the targets by *Oboe* or *H2S*-equipped Mosquitoes from No. 8 Group. Typical of these operations was No. 692 and No. 571 Squadrons' raid on Berlin on the night of 13/14 April 1944. This was the first time B. XVIs, carrying drop tanks and the 4,000 lb bomb, had attacked the capital. In the face of a heavy weather front over much of Germany, the force had to climb to over 28,000 feet to cross it. *Oboe*-equipped 139 Squadron dropped T.Is. a few minutes late, which forced 692 Squadron, equipped with 4,000 lb bombs, to circle the city accompanied by hundreds of searchlights and moderate Flak.

Even with its improved speed and electronic aids, the Mosquito was not immune from fighter attack. Typical of such attacks was that experienced by a 692 Squadron B. XVI sent to Berlin on the night of 18/19 July 1944. At 0207 hours, at 26,000 feet over the capital, this Mosquito crew encountered the *Luftwaffe's* first true dedicated night-

fighter, the Heinkel He 219: '*A/C was coned in search lights on run to target for 2 mins before enemy fighter, believed He 219, attacked from dead astern and slightly below, firing a long burst of cannon and machine gun fire from 300–400 yds, which went straight over our a/c which then did a violent dive to port. Enemy aircraft not seen again.*' Lucky indeed, for the Heinkel carried a formidable battery of armament.

Even with two-stage Merlins in the B.XVI, caution had to be exercised on take-off if laden with the '4,000-pounder', due to the weight of the bomb and fuel load. It was wise to use as much of the runway as possible in order to gain maximum flying speed should an engine fail. The bomb could explode with a heavy impact such as a belly landing whether the bomb was fused or not! The 'cookie'-equipped B. XVI became the mainstay of Mosquito squadrons within Bomber Command, especially the LNSF, and these squadrons conducted numerous operations over Germany in the latter part of the war. These operations constituted not only conventional bombing but also mine-laying in the Kiel Canal as well as efforts to halt von Rundstedt's forces in western Germany by 'tossing' delayed-action 4,000 lb bombs into railway tunnels, although these were attempted with mixed results. In 1945 Berlin became an important target with nightly Mosquito raids to the capital often dubbed as 'milk runs' due to the regularity of operations. These raids utilised not only the LNSF but Squadrons from 8 Group as well. They culminated on the night of 21/22 March 1945 when 138 Mosquitoes from eight squadrons attacked Berlin in two waves – the largest ever Mosquito attack on the capital, in which only one aircraft was lost, B. XVI, PF392, P3-R from 692 Squadron, flown by W/O I. M. Macphee and Sgt A. V. Sullivan. The night of 2/3 May saw the last Bomber Command Mosquito attack of the war when 116 Mosquitoes from eight squadrons attacked Kiel in two waves.

Reichsmarschall Hermann Göring, Commander-in-Chief of the Luftwaffe, who is purported to have said amongst other things that the Mosquito made him 'turn green and yellow with envy'.

'Grace with pace', well known, but beautiful photograph of B. XVI, 8K-K, ML963 of 571 Squadron PFF, aloft whilst undergoing refurbishment at Hatfield. The aircraft was originally delivered to 109 Squadron on 9 March 1944, but then moved to 692 Squadron later in March. In April 1944 it passed to 571 Squadron, part of the LNSF and remained there on operations until early July 1944, when it then spent three months at Hatfield, undergoing repair. It resumed operations with 571 in October and continued to fly until 10 April 1945, when it sadly failed to return from an operation on Berlin.

The last Mosquito bomber type, the B. 35, an improved B. XVI with Merlin 113/114 engines was introduced too late to see service in the war – first flying on 12 March 1945. Like the B. XVI, it was built to carry the 4,000 lb bomb. This final mark was operated well into the early 1950s in the RAF (until replaced by the Canberra) and many were later modified to become TT. 35s (target tugs) and saw service in CAAU (civilian anti-aircraft units). A good number of surviving Mosquitoes are B. 35 airframes.

Raw statistics reveal that No. 8 (PFF) Group bomber Mosquitoes alone flew just under 27,000 operations during the war with 108 failing to return – a loss rate of only 0.63%, the lowest in Bomber Command. In total, from surviving figures for Bomber Command, some 40,000 Mosquito sorties were flown with a very credible 26,867 tons of bombs dropped, 10,000 of these being 4,000 lb

Cookies. From an aircraft at the beginning of the campaign that was somewhat unwanted by higher authorities in Bomber Command, it grew into a much valued and respected machine, loved by its crews and hated by the Germans. Ironically, perhaps the last words (often quoted) should be those purportedly of *Reichsmarschall* Hermann Göring, from 1943 to his deputy, Erhard Milch: '*In 1940 I could at least fly as far as Glasgow in most of my aircraft, but not now! It makes me furious when I see the Mosquito. I turn green and yellow with envy. The British, who can afford aluminium better than we can, knock together a beautiful wooden aircraft that every piano factory over there is building, and they give it a speed which they have now increased yet again. What do you make of that? There is nothing the British do not have. They have the geniuses and we have the nincompoops. After the war is over I'm going to buy a British radio set – then at least I'll own something that has always worked.*'

Left: A B. 35, the last Mosquito bomber variant. It was powered by two-stage Merlin 113/114s, with a pressure cabin and enlarged bomb bay as standard. Too late to see service in the war, many served post-war in the RAF until the early 1950s. Subsequently many were converted to Target Tugs - TT. 35s - and saw use well into the early 1960s. Some found stardom on the big screen in the '633 Squadron' and 'Mosquito Squadron' motion picture films. Many were sold into private ownership in the 1950s for use in the aerial-mapping role in North America, Spartan Air Services Ltd in Canada being one of the largest users. TK623 (left), was one such Mosquito – becoming CF-HMM with Spartan in 1955. CF-HMM fatally crashed on 27 March 1960 in the Dominican Republic.

Left: Surely the most bizarre looking Mosquito ever! The TT. 39 (Target Tug 39) was developed from the B. XVI and fulfilled the target-tug role within the Royal Navy post-war. Twenty-six were built, including two prototypes. A number were converted from Percival-built B. XVIs (see page 63). The example here TT. 39, PF606 was the only version to have four-bladed propellers and was converted by General Aircraft at Feltham and used for radio trials until SOC on 27 November 1952 at Lossiemouth. A camera operator was contained within the extensively glazed nose and there was also a rear dorsal 'turret' or cupola aft of the trailing edge of the wing which housed another observer/drogue operator who faced towards the rear. Drogue targets were streamed from a hydraulically-powered winch in the bomb bay, which was powered by a retractable propeller.
(Stephen Skinner)

Above: Canada was a big producer of Mosquitoes during the war - in total 1,034 were manufactured there, around 400 of which were the B. XXV with Packard Merlin 225s, like KB557 above, which saw service with the RAF with 162 Squadron. This Mosquito was SOC on 7 November 1947.

Mosquito B. XXV, KB377, CF-FZG - WORLD WIDE AIRWAYS - September 1948
In post-war North America, Mosquitoes became popular for air racing. A Canadian, Don McVicar from World Wide Aviation
(a very experienced wartime Atlantic ferry pilot on Mosquitoes), bought two war surplus Downsview-built B. XXVs, KB337 and KA984, from
War Assets Corp. for a bargain price of around $1500 each. The Mosquitoes were delivered to Dorval Airport on 2 July 1948. McVicar kept
KB337 for himself to go racing and sold KA984 to his friend, Jesse Stallings of Capitol Airways Inc., who wished to do likewise. Both McVicar
and Stallings entered their Mosquitoes in the 1948 Bendix Air Race from Long Beach to Cleveland. KB337 soon lost its wartime camouflage
and was repainted cream and green with the race number 41 and civil registration CF-FZG. Flying out to California, McVicar and Tom Colahan
(engineer) got as far as Wichita on 3 September when the starboard Merlin blew a connecting rod, forcing them out. Stallings finished fifth
in the Bendix on 4 September. McVicar later sold FZG to Donald Bussart of Illinois, and it became N37878. Bussart had Stallings prepare his
Mosquito for the 1949 Bendix, painted dark blue and cream with red triangles on the spinners with race number 81 on the fuselage – it came
fourth. It was then sold to Mark Hurd Co. to be modified for aerial photography in 1951, but was written off in a ground accident when an air
bottle being refilled in the fuselage exploded, blowing a large hole in the fuselage at MacCarron Field, Las Vegas, Nevada.

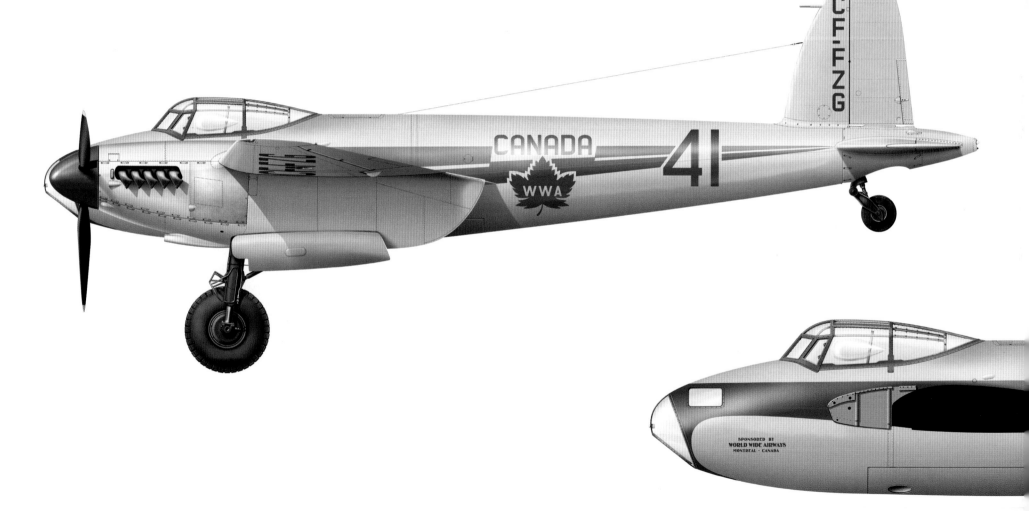

Below: A quick glance and it looks very much like a Mosquito – but they are radial engines powering this look-alike. This is an Argentinian I.Ae.24 Calquin. Designed by the Instituto Aerotécnico as a light tactical bomber, it was Argentina's first home-grown twin-engine design. The Mosquito B. IV very much inspired the design team, not only in appearance but in materials: it was made of wood with fabric-covered flying surfaces. Originally proposed to be powered by Merlins, these were unavailable, so Pratt & Whitney R-1830-G 'Twin Wasp' radials were used instead. These were underpowered compared to the Merlins envisaged and the aircraft was a poor performer. The first one flew in 1947, with more than 100 aircraft completed by 1950. Half of these were lost with their crews in accidents, partly attributed to its poor handling characteristics,
due to the low powered engines. The remaining Calquins served

FLYING ACES

MORE PICTURES • BETTER PICTURES

JUNE 15¢

SCHOMBURG

DE HAVILLAND MOSQUITO
ALL-WOOD FIGHTER-BOMBER

FOR VICTORY
BUY WAR BONDS
AND STAMPS

For many people in North America, both civilian and military alike, the front cover image from the June 1943 issue of 'Flying Aces', was probably their first glimpse of de Havilland's Mosquito, most likely based on the in-flight photographs of DZ313 (see page 54). The magazine was a mixture of contemporary and historic aviation articles with chapters on modelling – with a good dose of propaganda thrown in! Nevertheless it shows an extremely advanced and well established aircraft modelling industry in the US during the war with a plethora of kits of both Allied and Axis aircraft for scratch-building or ready-to-make kits. Some were very accurate for the day and others not so – see opposite page.
(Michael Davies)

The Mosquito has remained a firm favourite with modellers for many years. The simple plans below for a scratch-built Bomber B. IV out of wood, are probably the very first commercially available – found in the US wartime magazine 'Flying Aces' in 1943 (opposite page). Whilst the accuracy of the actual aircraft is open to question (the cover art on the magazine is more accurate!), it would appear that the colour scheme is based on a 105 Squadron machine. (Michael Davies)

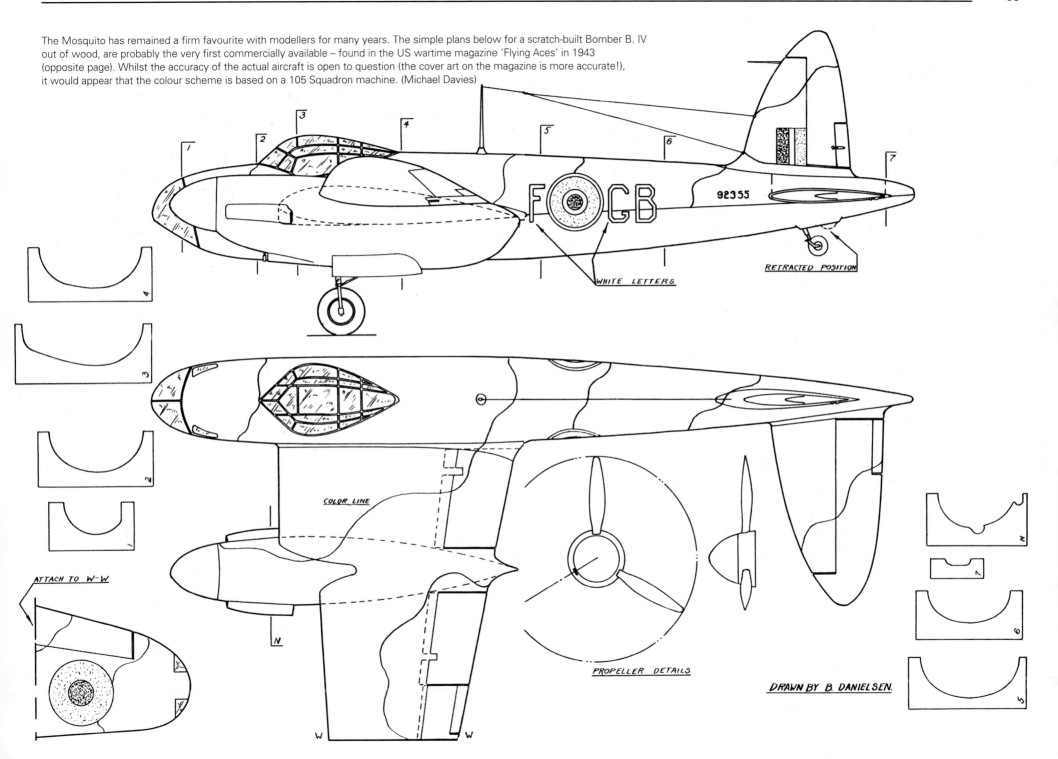

WHITE LETTERS

RETRACTED POSITION

ATTACH TO W-W

COLOR LINE

PROPELLER DETAILS

DRAWN BY B. DANIELSEN.

'SPEED BIRD' TO SWEDEN 6

THE story of the Mosquito cannot be told without including its wartime service with BOAC (British Overseas Airways Corporation) as a fast, unarmed, courier and improvised passenger aircraft. Before the war British Airways Ltd (BAL) had commenced a weekly service between the British Isles, Norway, Sweden and Finland. Apart from Paris this was the only civil route still being flown that was to continue after 3 September 1939 when Britain declared war on Germany. Due to hostilities between Russia and Finland during the 'Winter War' (November 1939 to March 1940), the route had to be curtailed at Stockholm and, come the morning of 9 April 1940, with the German invasion of Norway and Denmark, all flying was cancelled from Perth in Scotland. The airline at that time was using a mix of Lockheed 14s and, ironically, German Junkers Ju 52s – the very aircraft the *Luftwaffe* was using for its *Fallschirmjäger* (paratroops) during the invasion. From March 1940 all flying was transferred from BAL to BOAC.

Very little flying was done for the rest of the year, with only nine direct flights to Stockholm.

Yet the need for a regular service to Sweden was clear: it was soon to become the only neutral country in North West Europe. Communication had to remain open for Britain, otherwise Sweden's influence could have been surrendered to Germany, which was keen to retain contact with its Scandinavian neighbour, particularly with facilitating troop movements and acquiring raw materials. Sweden retained the cable for all outside communication but, if *personal* communication was to remain open, it had to be facilitated by air. Equally, Britain could send Government officials and diplomats to assert its continuing presence in a Europe overrun by Nazi Germany. More importantly, Sweden produced some of the finest ball-bearings in the world and it was vital that Britain should acquire them and at the same time prevent Germany from having them. Every mechanical instrument of war (or peace) will contain, within it somewhere, ball-bearings. Without them, there is no war.

From 1941, the daylight route was particularly dangerous for these civil aircraft, which were a mixture of Hudsons, Lodestars, DC-3s and converted Whitley bombers, the latter very unpopular with their

Left: A BOAC Mosquito FB. VI comes in to land at Leuchars in Scotland, the airline's base for the flights to Sweden. Believed to be G-AGGD, HJ681, this unarmed fighter-bomber was the second FB. VI to be delivered to the airline on 16/17 April 1943. It lasted eight-and-a-half months with the airline, suffering severe damage in a heavy landing on 3 January 1944 and reduced to spares. The crew were uninjured. Most if not all of the BOAC Mosquitoes flew with unshrouded exhausts – this gave them a useful increase in speed. (via David Vincent)

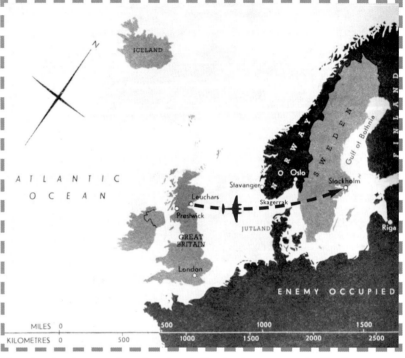

Map showing the route from Leuchars in Scotland, out across the North Sea and over the Skagerrak to Sweden. The Skagerrak was flanked by the enemy-held coasts of Norway and Denmark, which made the flights dangerous due to the attentions of the Luftwaffe and coastal Flak.

crews. They flew from Leuchars, the preferred Scottish base for the Stockholm route, out across the North Sea to the Skagerrak, a large body of water flanked by Norway and Denmark. To this site the Germans had moved anti-aircraft batteries and radio detection equipment and established *Luftwaffe* fighter bases. The BOAC crews were a mixture of Polish, Norwegian and British nationals, and they had to fly the route as high as possible at night. In these northern latitudes this sometimes involved moonlight, Northern Lights and in summer, due to the long twilight, little darkness at all. To minimise the chance of interception at these heights, oxygen was required for crew and passengers, depending on aircraft type.

FB. VI, G-AGGF, runs up her Merlins prior to a dusk departure from Leuchars in Scotland bound for Sweden. This aircraft was sadly to become the airline's first Mosquito loss after only four months' service. It crashed on 17 August 1943, in bad weather on approach after aborting its mission soon after take-off. Capt Wilkens and his Radio Officer, N. Beaumont, were killed. Capt Wilkens headed up the Mosquito operations as Flight Captain and his loss was keenly felt.

In late 1942 came a revolutionary change with the adoption of the Mosquito on the Swedish run. It had been pioneered by a B. IV Mosquito from 105 Squadron, devoid of military markings, with crew in civilian dress who had made a secret run to Sweden with mail on 6 August 1942, for the RAF. The Mosquito's speed and height capability gave it a good chance of avoiding interception so thoughts turned to using the aircraft in daylight. Due to its small size and lack of a passenger cabin it was used to take diplomatic mail, newspapers and magazines to Sweden and bring back ball-bearings in baskets, suspended from hooks in the bomb bay, which was filled to capacity.

BOAC used two types of converted Mosquitoes, one B. IV

and ten FB. VIs. The faster B. IV was always the favourite with the BOAC crews and was the first type (registered G-AGFV, serial DZ411) to be delivered for service with the airline on 15 December 1942. It flew its maiden Stockholm run on 4 February 1943, crewed by Captain C. Houlder and Radio Officer Frape. It was this aircraft, flown by Captain Gilbert Rae which, on the night of 22/23 April 1943, whilst returning from Stockholm at 17,000 feet over the Skagerrak was intercepted by an Fw 190 from astern. Captain Rae used the aircraft's speed to escape, but it was hit by cannon fire and the starboard wing and fuselage were holed, the hydraulics badly damaged, and the escape hatch shot off, sucking out all the maps and everything movable from the cockpit. Rae turned back for Sweden, to make a successful belly-landing at an airfield north of Stockholm at more than 120 mph due to his undercarriage and flaps not working. Though damaged, his aircraft was in time repaired and back in service. This attack was a response from the Germans who had bolstered their defences against these incursions by moving fighter units into the area. It was after this that a pause in operations occurred whilst six unarmed FB. VIs were acquired and the Mosquitoes switched to night flights, which continued through the summer of 1943.

B. IV, DZ411, G-AGFV at Leuchars in 1943. It was the first Mosquito delivered to BOAC on 15 December 1942 and was also the only B. IV to be used by the airline, the rest being unarmed FB. VI. On the night of 22/23 April 1943, whilst flying across the Skagerrak, this Mosquito was attacked by an Fw 190 which damaged the aircraft forcing it to belly land near Stockholm. It took around eight months to repair and was back on operations on 10 December 1943. After just over two years of service this Mosquito was returned to the RAF on 6 January 1945. (Brian Doherty)

A tight fit in the aft bomb bay for a passenger in a BOAC Mosquito. Although rather unorthodox, this was a successful method by which British Intelligence and the Government were able to transport important individuals out of Sweden via the occupied countries and occasionally to Sweden from Britain when important diplomatic missions had to take place.

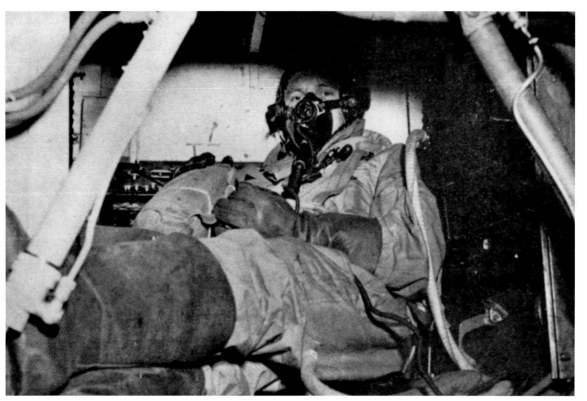

There then came an urgent demand in late June from the Air Ministry that two diplomats had to be flown to Sweden. They had to be in Stockholm the following morning to counter a German move to secure all the ball-bearings for the German war effort – prompted, in part, by the Allied bombing raids on the ball-bearing factories in Germany. The only way to transport a passenger in a Mosquito was in the bomb-bay of the aircraft, accessed from the outside via the bomb doors, but with no access to the inside of the machine. The passenger would be entirely alone, able only to recline. The bomb bays of two Mosquitoes were padded with felt and equipped with safety belts. Each passenger, dressed in full flying clothing, was strapped in so the bomb bay doors could be shut. The passenger could then stretch his legs, communicate with the pilots via RT, eat a sandwich with a flask of coffee and read a book using a light – definitely not the kind of service BOAC passengers had to enjoy ordinarily! One can only imagine being in that confined space with no window, with little sound deadening, the loud din of the

two Merlins crackling away and the jolts and movement associated with the flight, knowing that if anything went wrong, the chance of survival was very slim. But it had to be done and in this manner the diplomats were taken to Stockholm in less than three hours, compared to the nine hours previously taken in the slower aircraft. The two passengers were brought back a few nights later having succeeded in their diplomatic mission.

Eventually this led to more passengers being transported and some notable personages travelled this way – often oblivious to the manoeuvres the aircraft had to undertake to avoid interception and Flak. Not so on the night of 18 July 1943, when Captain Gilbert Rae and his Radio Officer, J. Payne, in Mosquito G-AGGC were intercepted, Scotland-bound in bright moonlight, just off the Swedish coast, by two German fighters. Procedure demanded that if intercepted homeward-bound and still over the Skagerrak, they were to turn back for Sweden, but Rae knew he had an important passenger aboard, whom the Germans had asked the Swedes to hand over prior to the flight. Contrails from the two fighters, presumed to be Fw 190s, were spotted at 23,000 feet in the bright moonlight. Rae jettisoned his wing tanks, put the nose down hard and dived to sea-level, weaving as he did so at full throttle. Gradually, he was able to pull away from the fighters and after 30 minutes they gave up the chase; but so violent was the evasive action that Payne was thrown about the cockpit and needed two weeks to recover from his injuries. When it appeared that the danger was over Rae called up the passenger to see how he was – there was no reply. He had passed out and remained in such a state for 20 minutes, but he had recovered sufficiently by the time that the

Mosquito landed back at Leuchars. It was surmised after this incident that German Intelligence knew about Rae's departure and passenger.

These flights were not without loss – even when using the Mosquito. On 17 August 1943 Captain Wilkins with his Radio Officer, N. Beaumont, left Leuchars in Mosquito G-AGGF, but soon radioed that he was returning. He never did. Three weeks later the wreckage of G-AGGF was found on the side of a mountain in Scotland – bad weather had claimed it. This was a sad loss as Wilkins had headed the whole operation and was BOAC's first Mosquito loss. These losses continued when Mosquito G-AGGG, flown by Captain Martin Hamre and Radio Officer Serre Haug, and a passenger crashed not far from home, after a long struggle back from Stockholm on one engine, on 25 October – little more than a month after the first tragedy. These losses were keenly felt in a civil airline not used to such frequent tragedy – war or no war.

In early 1944, a Captain John H. White made a series of remarkable flights that fully demonstrated the Mosquito's versatility. In nine hours he flew three journeys, on instruments at night and totalling 2,400 miles, with only three-quarters of an hour on the ground. A peak in Mosquito flights was reached in 1944, with 151 round trips made between May and August that year. June was the busiest month, with 42 flights alone. Yet even with the invasion of Europe on 6 June 1944 and the gradual redefining of Nazi Germany's hold on Europe by the Allied armies, the flights continued but alas, also the losses. Captain Gilbert Rae who had achieved and experienced so much behind the controls of a Mosquito, which had earned him an OBE, was lost together with his Radio Officer, D. Roberts, and a fellow Captain, B. Orton, as a passenger, on the night of 18/19 August 1944. Flying Mosquito G-AGKP, they came down in the sea not far from Leuchars in good weather from unknown causes. Ten days later on 28/29 August, Captain John H. White (of record flight fame) and Radio Officer J. Gaffney were lost from unknown causes in Mosquito G-AGKR whilst returning from Göteborg.

In early November 1944, with an improving situation on the Allied front in western Europe, London decreed suspension of the flights in the winter months so as to avoid unnecessary risk. Only eight flights were made in this month, with service officially suspended on 30 November. There were only sporadic flights until 17 May 1945, when BOAC Mosquito flights officially came to an end.

From April 1943 to March 1945 BOAC Mosquitoes flew 783,680 miles, averaging nine trips per week. Out of the 14

Capt Gilbert Rae OBE, at the controls of an unarmed FB. VI. A very experienced pilot with BOAC, he was to survive many brushes with the Luftwaffe on the run to Sweden. Sadly, he was to lose his life with his Radio Officer D. Roberts and a fellow Captain, B. Orton, on the night of 18/19 August 1944, when their Mosquito G-AGKP came down in the sea in good weather to unknown causes.

Mosquitoes used by BOAC (three of which were T.IIIs), four were lost on operations with their crews and two passengers. This has to count as a remarkable achievement by an unarmed wooden aircraft in a time of war – made more so by the spirit and determination of the crews who flew and maintained them.

BOAC Mosquito FB. VI, G-AGGC, HJ680

Delivered on 16 April 1943, G-AGGC, was the first unarmed FB. VI for the airline and subsequently proved to be the longest serving Mosquito with BOAC, with 33 months of service. This Mosquito, flown by Capt Gilbert Rae OBE and his R/O, J. Payne, survived a notable moonlight encounter with two Fw 190s on 18 August 1943 whilst carrying an important passenger. It was returned to the RAF on 9 January 1946 and sold for scrap on 16 June 1950.

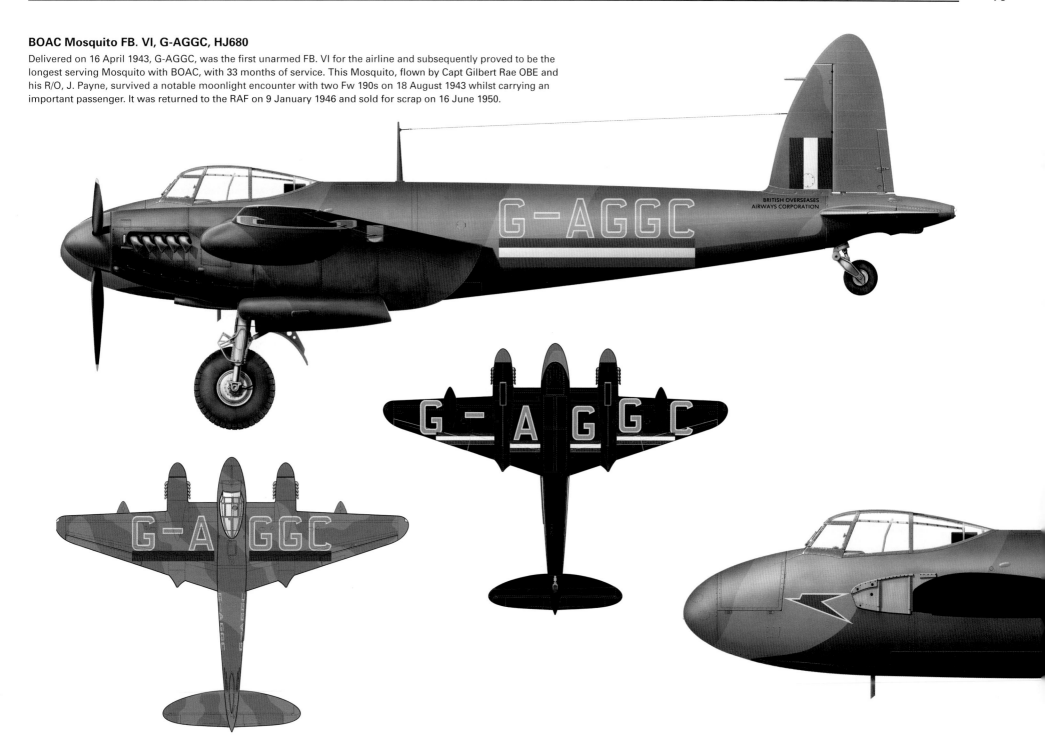

HUNTING IN THE DARK 7

The Bristol Beaufighter (above) shared in the early defence of the night skies of Britain in its radar-equipped versions, prior to the Mosquito. In some cases the Beaufighter was the better aircraft due to its stronger construction and air cooled Hercules radial engines which were less sensitive to combat damage unlike the liquid-cooled Merlins. Nevertheless, many Beaufighter squadrons became all-Mosquito units in time though later marks of Beaufighter night-fighters and anti-shipping/torpedo marks continued to play their part to the end of the war with great success.

Left: The prototype Mosquito night-fighter W4052. Like the bomber prototype, it was built at Salisbury Hall but unlike W4050, it was flown out of the Hall on 15 May 1941. It carries the original exhaust cowling design and has A.I. Mk. IV radar fitted and is painted in all-over RDM 2A Special Night Finish, known as 'Lamp Black'.

THE second prototype Mosquito to be built was W4052, built to the Specification of F 21.40 – a night-fighter. Like the bomber prototype it was built at Salisbury Hall, but unlike the bomber it flew out from a field adjacent to the Hall in the capable hands of Geoffrey de Havilland Jr. on 15 May 1941. A field hedge had been removed for the take-off run, much to the annoyance of a local farmer. This alternative route saved much time as it negated the need to dismantle the aircraft, transport it to Hatfield by road, reassemble it and resume flight-testing. Such was the urgency in a country that was at war and at this stage quite alone. W4052 was essentially the fighter version (an F. II) armed with four nose-mounted .303 Browning machine guns and four 20 mm Hispano cannon beneath the nose with the essential fitment of the first generation of British-designed airborne radar for its night role – the ultra secret A.I. or Air Intercept Mk IV radar. The aircraft also had strengthened wing spars to meet the loads imposed as a fighter. Like all early RAF night-fighters, it was finished in an all-over RDM 2A Special Night Finish, popularly known as 'Lamp Black', which formed the accepted thinking for night camouflage at the time, although this had a penalty in slowing the aircraft by around 23 mph. Like the bomber, the fighter prototype experienced teething troubles with its exhaust flame dampeners and attendant cowling blistering. Flight trials at night with the prototype also saw the need for flash eliminators to be fitted to the .303s on production NF. IIs so as to avoid the crew losing their night vision.

Britain's early attempts at night interception during the latter half of the Battle of Britain and the Blitz had been achieved by the use of single-engine day fighters (Spitfires, Hurricanes, Defiants) and radar-equipped Blenheims with very mixed, if not poor, results especially compared with the new radar-equipped twin-engine Beaufighter. The Beaufighter had only been available in limited numbers during the Battle of Britain and first saw use at the newly established FIU (Fighter Interception Unit) at Tangmere, 12 August 1940. Five RAF squadrons were each equipped with a single Beaufighter in September, but never managed to become fully

operational by the end of the battle in October. The first A.I. Beaufighter victory was not until 19/20 November 1940, when F/L Cunningham, who later became a Mosquito night-fighter ace – shot down a Ju 88. The need for the NF. II version of the F. II Mosquito to assume operations became urgent when, in early 1942, the *Luftwaffe* began a new night-bombing campaign over the UK known as the '*Baedeker* raids'.

In January 1942 No. 157 Squadron took delivery of the first Mosquito night-fighter at Castle Camps in Cambridgeshire along with a dual-control T. III to assist in pilot conversion. The unit's first night operational sortie was on 27/28 April when three Mosquitoes made patrols – without contact, as it happened – but the pressure was on. It was not until a month later on the night of 29/30 May that the Mosquito began to hit back; Squadron Leader Ashfield in NF. II, W4099 of 157 Squadron made contact with a Dornier Do 217 E-4 whilst patrolling the Channel south of Dover and claimed it as a probable. Two other Mosquitoes from another early night-fighter unit, No. 151 Squadron, made contact with Do 217 E-4s with claims of damage. Another unit to convert to the NF. II was No. 264 Squadron based at Colerne. This unit claimed a Do 217 E-4 of KG 40, part of a force that raided Nuneaton, on the night of 24/25 June. 151 Squadron made its first confirmed victories on the night of 25/26 June with two Mosquitoes from the unit claiming a Heinkel He 111 H and a Do 217 E-4 respectively. Sqdn Ldr Ashfield finally opened the score for his unit with a He 111 over the North Sea on 27/28 July.

As mentioned, Mosquito night-fighters up to this time had been painted 'Lamp Black' but this soon changed to Smooth Night

The first generation of British airborne radar, A.I. Mk.IV, first seen on the NF. II Mosquito. (David Wadman)

Continued on page 82

Left: A superb study of the night-fighter prototype W4052, tucking up her wheels as she takes off. It now wears the now standard night-fighter finish of medium sea grey overall with a disruptive pattern of dark green on the upper surfaces. Note that the radar has been removed and that she carries production exhausts, unshrouded in this case as part of a continuing trials programme. W4052 eventually joined the FIU at Ford and this famous aircraft was scrapped on 28 January 1946.

Right: DD739 was built as an F. II at Hatfield, before conversion to an NF. II and served with 85 Squadron, before passing to 456 Squadron RAAF coded RX-X. Like a lot of NF. IIs it was eventually shorn of radar and used for Ranger and night intruder work. It is seen here being flown by F/L Col Griffin from Adelaide, when 456 was based at Middle Wallop (from March to August 1943). Col joined 456 in late 1942 (see page 7) and survived the war – he still regularly flies his high performance RV-6 sports aircraft. DD739 went missing on a bomber support mission to Kassel on 4 December 1943. (Stephen Lewis/Bob Cowper)

Left: A contemporary of the early Mosquito F. IIs was the twin-engine Westland Whirlwind. Like the Mosquito fighter it packed a heavy punch with its four cannon and was powered by Rolls-Royce engines – in this case the R-R Peregrine. It made a superb ground-attack aircraft and was a delight to fly, though its performance fell off at altitude. Continued problems with the Peregrine and other factors kept numbers low and the aircraft ceased operations in 1943. One Whirlwind (P6972) was tested as a night-fighter in 1940 with No. 25 Squadron.

Above and left: de Havilland Mosquito NF. II, DD750, in-flight and probably at Hatfield, was an early example of the radar A.I. Mk. IV equipped variant and whose introduction in 1942 marked the beginning of the Mosquito fighter's career. Note how the censor in the above photograph has removed the radar aerials on the nose and wings. DD750 reached the RAF on 7 September 1942, and after installation of the radar was allocated to No. 151 Squadron on 6 October 1942, after which it was transferred to No. 264 Squadron on 29 July 1943 after having been used on Day Rangers. No.157 Squadron received it on 14 August 1943, operating it on a number of successful Insteps. No. 410 Squadron also used it and following overhaul it reached No. 239 Squadron on 25 April 1944. Whilst on operations on 28 June 1944, it was damaged beyond repair. (Photograph at left courtesy Flight International www.flightglobal.com)

FIG 1

INSTRUMENT PANEL

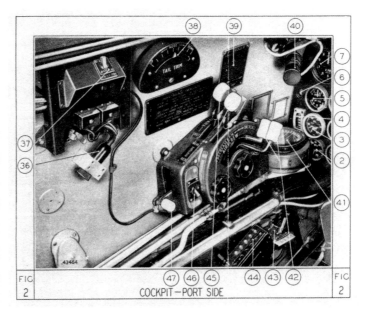

FIG 2

COCKPIT—PORT SIDE

FIG 3

COCKPIT—STARBOARD SIDE

NF./F. II cockpit (without radar).
(via David Wadman)

1. Landing Light switches
2. Coolant temperature gauges
3. Oil temperature gauges
4. Oil pressure gauges
5. Boost pressure gauges
6. Fuel pressure warning light
7. RPM indicators
8. Boost control cut-out
9. Instrument light
10. Gun sight
11. Instrument flying panel
12. Radiator flap switches
13. Rudder trimming tab control and indicator
14. Electrical services switch
15. Magneto switches
16. Engine electric starter switches
17. Booster coil switches

18. Immersed fuel pump warning light
19. Propeller feathering buttons
20. Ventilator
21. Undercarriage position indicator
22. Flaps position indicator
23. Undercarriage selector lever
24. Flaps selector lever
25. Gun master switch
26. Aileron trimming tab control and indicator
27. Windscreen de-icing pump
28. Camera gun button
29. Machine gun firing control
30. Cannon firing trigger
31. Control column
32. Brake control lever
33. Parking brake catch
34. Triple pressure gauge
35. Mark VIIIc oxygen regulator.

2. Coolant temperature gauges.
3. Oil temperature gauges.
4. Oil pressure gauges.
5. Boost pressure gauges.
6. Fuel pressure warning lights.
7. R.P.M. indicators.
36. Intercom jack.
37. Beam approach switch.
38. Elevator trimming tab indicator.
39. Engine limitations data plate.
40. Compass light.
41. Compass.
42. Propeller speed control levers.
43. Radio set-selector switch.
44. Radio control unit.
45. Throttle levers.
46. Supercharger gear change switch.
47. Mixture control lever (locked in WEAK position).
48. Emergency door-jettison handle.
49. Identification switch box and key.
50. Air recognition lights switch.
51. Identification lights selector switch.
52. Camera gun switch.
53. Navigation lights switch.
54. Ultra-violet lighting switch.
55. Pitot head heater switch.
56. Immersed fuel pump switch (if pump fitted).
57. Generator switch (not in use).
58. Navigation headlamp switch.
59. I.F.F. switch.
60. I.F.F. detonator buttons.
61. Fire extinguisher switches.
62. Fuel contents gauges.
63. Air temperature gauge.
64. High pressure oxygen master valve.
65. Mark VIIIc oxygen regulator.
66. Ventilation control.
67. Stowage for signal pistol.
68. Stowage for signal pistol cartridges.
69. Windscreen wiper rheostat.
70. Generator warning light.
71. Voltmeter.

Far left: The next generation of airborne radar to be fitted to Mosquitoes was the A.I. Mk. VIII, fitted to NF. IIs, which in turn became NF. XIIs (left). The fitment of this radar in the nose removed the four machine guns leaving only the four 20 mm cannon in the forward belly of the aircraft. This still proved quite sufficient! The radar fitted to the NF. XII was also found in the later NF. XIII. (A.I. Mk. VIII photograph David Wadman, NF. XII photograph via Stephen Skinner)

DTD308, although operational experience was to find this new 'black' scheme still wanting due to silhouetting of the aircraft in moonlight and above or below cloud in conditions of good visibility. From late 1942, effectively all night-fighters were to follow the colours of their daytime sisters but with retention of Smooth Night for under surfaces for some.

The improvement in radar technology was to see the night-fighting Mosquito NF. IIs develop into the NF. XIIs using A.I. Mk.VIII radar (these aircraft were converted NF. IIs). This new radar was housed in the nose in a 'thimble'-shaped radome and resulted in the removal of the nose-mounted machine guns, thus reducing the armament to the four cannon. These aircraft came on stream in late February 1943 with No. 151 Squadron and shortly after with No. 85 Squadron under the command of Wg Cdr John Cunningham. Mid-April 1943 was to see the first kills by NF. XIIs when 85 Squadron made claims for two Do 217 E-4s of II./KG 40 during a raid on Chelmsford. Soon after, the *Luftwaffe* deployed a new form of attack against Britain using Fw 190 A-4 and A-5 fighters from SKG 10, carrying a bomb beneath the fuselage and drop tanks under the wings. Their principal target was London and, predominantly, they came over at night, although daylight missions were also flown. Their first night raid ended up with three Focke-Wulfs landing in error at West Malling through faulty navigation, with a fourth crashing nearby! First to claim an Fw 190 at night was F/L H. E. 'Taps' Tappin of 157 Squadron based at Hudson in Essex. Two nights later 85 Squadron had great success with the first Fw 190s shot down at night over Britain after night-flying Hawker Typhoons sent up to combat the Fw 190s had failed to make contact. The Squadron diarist related: '*After an hour or so, it was clearly seen that the Typhoons were unable to cope so the 11 Gp Controller risked his bowler hat and grounded them thus enabling the 85 Sqn Mosquitoes to go in and deal with the 190s which they did in no uncertain manner. Sqn Ldr Green and Flt Sgt Grimstone were first to go to work. Under the control of Sandwich, they patrolled the Channel for some time at 10,000 feet and then having got a*

A Focke-Wulf Fw 190 A-5 of an unidentified unit loaded with an SC 500 kg bomb and two 300 ltr auxiliary fuel tanks. This was the type of aircraft and bomb load carried by Fw 190s of SKG 10.

Far left: F/L 'Taps' Tappin (left) and Plt Off Thomas of 157 Squadron, photographed by their Mosquito, claimed the first Fw 190 at night from 1./SKG 10 over France on 14/15 May 1943. (Chris Goss)

vector of 040 degrees increased height to 18,000 feet. Pilot got a contact at the miles range and closing rapidly got a visual at 1,000 feet range of an Fw 190 with long-range tanks and a bomb under the fuselage. Pilot opened fire with a short burst from dead astern at 100 yards range whereupon the e/a blew up with a large red flash, the Mosquito having to dive sharply to port to avoid the burning debris… They have the honour of being the first night-fighters to shoot down an Fw 190 over this country at night. They also landed the prizes that had been offered for the first Fw 190 which were as follows: £5 from F/L Molony, a bottle of gin from Wg Cdr Cunningham, a bottle of champagne from Sqn Ldr Crew and a bottle of whiskey from Sqn Ldr Green. Also a silver model of a Mosquito (for the Sqn) from Sqn Ldr Bradshaw-Jones… Not a bad night's work.'[1]

During some lulls in the fighting many night-fighter Mosquitoes, using NF. IIs, indulged in *Ranger* operations over France at night. Known as 'Night Rangers', they roamed a specific area using their own initiative to seek out any targets of opportunity instead of attacking a predetermined target. Often these took the form of *Luftwaffe* airfields, where the Mosquitoes would shoot down aircraft

---

[1.] *Luftwaffe Hit-and-Run Raiders*, Chris Goss, Classic Publications, London, 2008.

Aircrew of 85 Squadron around the time they began encountering the Fw 190s of I./SKG 10. Those identified who were successful against the Fw 190s are Bernard Thwaites (sitting far left), Bill Green (sitting second left), Bill Maguire (sitting second right) and Bob Robb (standing far right). (Chris Goss)

Mosquito NF. XIIIs of 96 Squadron at dispersal. The NF. XIII was a development using the FB. VI wing incorporating A.I. Mk. VIII radar The stronger wing of the fighter-bomber enabled this Mosquito to take drop tanks or wing-mounted bombs on their offensive incursions. (Chris Goss)

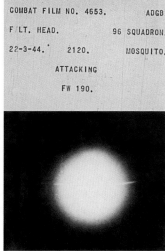

COMBAT FILM NO. 4653.　　　ADGB.

F/LT. HEAD.　　　96 SQUADRON.

22-3-44.　　2120.　　MOSQUITO.

ATTACKING

FW 190.

F/L Norman Head of 96 Squadron. A Mosquito night-fighter pilot, he would survive the war with four enemy aircraft destroyed and two probables, of which two of the destroyed were Fw 190s from I./SKG 10. The photograph above right shows an Fw 190 G-2 through the camera-gun of F/L Norman Head's Mosquito, the moment it exploded on 22 March 1944. (Chris Goss)

operating in the circuit, often in full view of the airfield. These NF. IIs were stripped of A.I. radar as it was not allowed on ops over France, lest the radar's secrets fall into German hands. In time, as the A.I. radar was superseded, it was released for operation over the continent but the radar found in the NF. XII and later marks was not released for operations over the continent until 1944.

January 1943 was to see another new type of radar installed in Mosquitoes: SCR 720 (A.I. Mk. X to the RAF). This was a US development of British radar. NF. IIs were in turn converted to take the new radar, which was contained within a large radome commonly called Universal ('Bull') Nose. These new mark Mosquitoes were re-designated NF. XVIIs and appeared on operations in late 1943. Alongside these NF. XVII and NF. XIIs in late 1943 came yet another new night-fighter, based on the FB.VI wing – the NF. XIII with A.I. Mk.VIII radar. With the stronger wing of the fighter-bomber, these new night-fighters could use their radar as well as wing-mounted ordnance or drop tanks on long-range interdictions over enemy territory at night. Later developments of the FB.VI with the improved Merlin 25s resulted in yet another night-fighter development: the NF. XIX using SCR 720. Alongside NF. XVIIs,

these Mosquitoes proved highly effective against the *Luftwaffe* during its 'Baby Blitz' (Operation *Steinbock*) bombing raids on London during early 1944. Even the use of '*Düppel*', the German equivalent of 'Window', in an attempt to jam British radar, especially against the A.I. Mk. X, proved futile.

By this time the Mosquito was operating in just about every conceivable role but as a night-fighter it attained new heights, especially as part of No. 100 (Bomber Support) Group, which was formed on 8 November 1943 to control radio countermeasures from the air and ground and to develop methods of protecting Bomber Command aircraft. If there was one arm of the *Luftwaffe* to reign supreme almost to the end of the war it was the night-fighter force – the *Nachtjagdwaffe*. From a slow beginning in 1940, it grew into an effective and extremely well organised arm of the *Luftwaffe* and took a very heavy toll of RAF Bomber Command aircraft on its nightly bombing operations over Germany as well as the occasional intruder operations over the UK. The *Nachtjäger* were to boast a string of aces, all of whom had perfected the art of flying in pitch-dark skies using effective ground control and radar to attain impressive individual victory scores. Into this maelstrom entered the Mosquito night-fighter and, in time, the hunter increasingly became the hunted. Equipped with suitably developed radar countermeasures, Mosquito night-fighters began reining in the *Nachtjäger* and soon almost every loss to the Germans was attributed to the Mosquito. Indeed some called it a '*Moskitopanik*'. Mosquito night-fighters carried a variety of radar countermeasures to use against the *Nachtjäger*: 'Serrate' – a device that could home in on *Luftwaffe* night-fighter radar transmissions; 'Perfectos' – for homing in on the enemy's Identification Friend or Foe (IFF) transmissions; and for the Mosquitoes' own protection, a tail warning radar called 'Monica'.

With the ever-increasing need for improved performance at altitude, de Havilland introduced the NF. 30 to operations on 13 June 1944. This was an NF. XIX airframe with Rolls-Royce Merlin 72 Two-Stage engines and A.I. Mk. X radar. The new aircraft was expected to operate as a long-range escort for Bomber Command operations which it did with great success after initial problems with the design of the exhaust shrouds.

After D-Day, night-fighting Mosquitoes were often patrolling the English Channel at night, offering protection to the Allied fleet from the *Luftwaffe*. Some attempted incursions took the form of Heinkel He 177 bombers and Dornier Do 217s carrying radio-guided, rocket-propelled glider bombs called Hs 293 A-1s. F/L Bob Cowper

Above and below: The final development of airborne radar to see service in the Mosquito during the war and post-war was the A.I. Mk. X (SCR 720). This was an American development of British radar and proved to be an excellent adaption of British technology. The photographs show the Indicator. This radar was fitted to the NF. XVII, NF. XIX, NF. XXX, NF. 36 and some NF. 38s post-war. Both the NF. XXX, NF. 36 and NF. 38 used two-stage Merlins. This radar with some minor modifications saw service up to 1961 in Meteors. (via David Wadman)

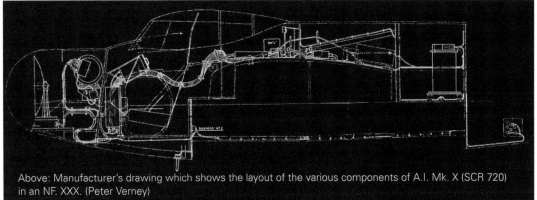

Above: Manufacturer's drawing which shows the layout of the various components of A.I. Mk. X (SCR 720) in an NF. XXX. (Peter Verney)

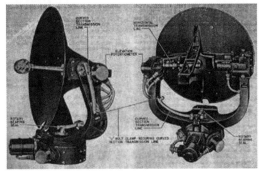

Above: Few photographs exist of A.I. Mk. X (SCR 720) in a Mosquito, but the image at top shows the 'bull' nose fairing with the access hatch removed showing the Radio Modulator Unit, but the antenna dish has been removed. The radar, a parabolic dish, can be seen above. The dish rotated continuously round its vertical and horizontal axis. This radar was a huge step over the previous A.I. Mk. VIII, which could only see 6.5 miles ahead and 1.9 miles to the side. SCR 720 could see 10 miles in front and to either side. It did nothing for the appearance of the Mosquito though, over earlier night-fighter versions – nevertheless this radar in the Mosquito made for a formidable combination in the night skies over Germany. (Peter Verney)

Experienced night fighter crew F/O Taffy Bellis and F/O Dennis Welfare of 239 Squadron stand by the tail of their Mosquito, damaged in combat when they (probably) shot down the last Fw 190 of I./SKG 10 on 9 August 1944 before the Luftwaffe unit was re-designated III./KG 51. Their combat report reads as follows: *'Mosquito crossed coast of France on way in at 2250 hrs. Patrol was uneventful so investigated target areas. On leaving them, height 11,000 feet for home, AI contact was obtained at 0005 hrs crossing from port to starboard 2,000 feet above. We turned on to this and chased for about 10 minutes closing in to 1500 feet but as the target was flying dead into moon only fleeting visuals were obtained on a single exhaust. After a further five minutes target was slightly to one side of moon and visual regained at 800 feet. On closing in to 3-400 feet, target was seen to be a s/e a/c with long-range tanks. Closing in to 200 feet, identified as a Fw 190 and shot it down at 0020 hrs near Ste Quentin. The Fw blew up in great style and also exploded very nicely on hitting the ground.'* 239 Squadron was originally an army co-operation unit and it changed to a night fighting role in early December 1943, when it received some NF. IIs at West Raynham. It was primarily in the bomber support role, escorting main force bomber operations, though sometimes it was involved in long-range intrusion sorties. The squadron used a mix force of NF. IIs and FB. VIs and flew its last NF. II operations in late October 1944. In January 1945 NF. XXXs joined the squadron and by May 1945 the unit had claimed 55 victories. The squadron was disbanded at West Raynham on 1 July 1945. (Chris Goss)

Above and below: NF. XIII Mosquitoes of 409 'Nighthawk' Squadron, RCAF. This was the RCAF's second night-fighter squadron to be formed overseas on 7 June 1941. It initially used Defiants and Beaufighters, before moving onto Mosquito NF. XIIIs in March 1944. It supported the Allied invasion and was the first night-fighter unit to be stationed on the Continent on 24 August 1944 at Carpiquet airfield. Note the airman taking a break on the port tailplane of KP–R, HK425 below. This Mosquito was formally KP–D with the squadron and known as 'Lonesome Polecat' (note the overpainted 'D' beneath the 'R'). On the night of 25/26 November 1944 F/O R. Britten and F/L L. Fownes shot down a Ju 88 and damaged another over Rheindahlen in KP–D and by the end of the war they had destroyed five aircraft. HK425 was SOC on 21 November 1945. Note that the NF. XIII in the above photograph has the Universal ('bull') nose and HK425 below has the 'thimble' nose. The NF. XIII came with both types of noses, but the same type of radar – the A.I. Mk. VIII. (David Wadman)

Right: Sqn Ldr Geoff Howitt, DFC of 456 Squadron caught by the camera at the bottom of the ladder of his NF. XVII, RX-B (fitted with A.I. Mk. X radar) after a flight. Note the camera gun housing on the side of the fuselage nose, forward of the crew access door. The circular plate below the nose is the radar scanner mount fairing. Note that the cannon remain faired over, indicating the flight was probably an air test. The circular blue and white disc on the access door was the squadron's unofficial emblem or crest – in this case uncompleted. It should have had a red kangaroo in the middle (see page 92). It was created by a squadron member whilst en route to Europe via ship – based on an old Australian penny coin. A version of this emblem was subsequently adopted as a roundel by the RAAF post-war for all its aircraft. (via David Vincent)

Above: With Luftwaffe high-altitude photo-reconnaissance/bomber aircraft operating with relative impunity over the British Isles in the early 1940s, the need for a high-altitude pressure cabin fighter was seen as paramount. MP469 was originally built as a bomber and served in pressure cabin trials. She was heavily modified for the fighter role with four machine guns in the nose, much lightening of the structure, extended wing tips, four-bladed propellers and small diameter wheels. Once modified she weighed 2,300 lbs less than an F. II and reached 43,500 feet on 14 September 1942. In time with the threat of the daylight high-altitude raider lessening, thoughts turned to combating the high-altitude night raider. MP469 was once again modified, with A. I. Mk. VIII radar in a thimble nose with the four machine guns relocated to a blister gun pack under the fuselage. With the added radar it could still reach 42,000 feet. Such was the perceived need for this type – four similar aircraft were built, known as the NF. XV. (David Wadman)

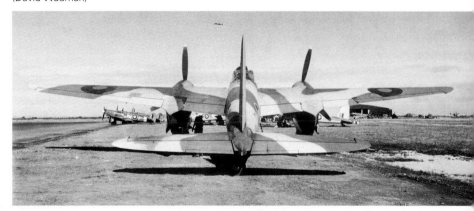

Above: Rear view showing the sleek lines of a Mosquito of 456 Squadron. (Bob Cowper)

of No. 456 (RAAF) Squadron flying out of Ford in Sussex recalled his unit's encounters with them:

'The glider bombs many of the German aircraft carried over the Normandy area were rocket propelled and radio-controlled. The aircraft carrying them could stand off from the ships they hoped to sink, and guide the bombs to their target, safe from anti-aircraft fire. The huge disadvantage of this was that they had to fly on nights when the moon gave them enough light to see their target, and this obviously made it easier for us to see them. As I recall, 456 Squadron pilots were responsible for shooting every one of the rocket-carrying aircraft from the skies.'

On the night of 10 June 1944 Bob Cowper and his radar operator/navigator, F O Bill Watson (RAF), were airborne in their NF. XVII over the Channel:

'We patrolled under Black Gang GCI on an E-W line, north of Cherbourg Peninsula. During the early stages of the patrol, contacts on two bogeys were investigated and identified as Mosquitoes. At approximately 0345, Controller advised us that there was a possibility of trade travelling SE, and that Window was being dropped. We were on a vector 280 at 4500 ft and were directed to 190 then 130. At 0400 Window was seen and a contact obtained on an aircraft moving approx. SE, height 4000ft and dropping Window. It was doing a gentle figure of eight turn, starting to port. Speed was increased and a visual obtained at 2000 ft, when the e/a opened fire from the rear turret. Immediately afterwards, pilot recognised e/a as a He 177 from the huge wingspan and very square high tail-fin. E/a carried two large glider bombs outboard of the engine nacelles. Rear gunner continued to "hosepipe" fire, not very accurately, throughout the engagement. No engine exhausts were visible, and glider bombs gave the effect at first of a 4-engined a/c. When pilot recognised e/a as He 177, he fired a 1-second burst at 800ft, obtaining strikes on the port wing. E/a turned steeply starboard and lost height; another 2-second burst obtained strikes on starboard, parallel to the coast, and another

Below: F/L Bob Cowper RAAF (right) and his navigator/radar operator, F/L Bill Watson RAF, from 456 Squadron, shot down a He 177 and a Do 217 on the night of 10 June 1944, off the invasion beaches of Normandy as related left. (Bob Cowper)

Left: A Heinkel He 177 silhouetted against an afternoon sky. After making radar contact and closing in, many Mosquito night-fighter crews would have seen this silhouetted sight at night in order to make a positive visual identification, before opening fire. He 177s carrying Hs 293 radio-controlled rocket-propelled glider-bombs were used at night by the Luftwaffe in an attempt to hit Allied vessels off the D-Day landing beaches – and themselves came under attack by Mosquito night-fighters, as related in the text above. The He 177, whilst giving the appearance of a twin-engine bomber, was in fact a four engine bomber. In each broad engine nacelle was a DB 610 engine (two conventional DB 605 V12s coupled together) driving a single large four-bladed propeller. The design was not one of Ernst Heinkel's success stories.

F/Lt R.B.COWPER, D.F.C, (R.A.A.F.)
F/O W.WATSON (R.A.F.)   S E C R E T

PILOT'S PERSONAL COMBAT REPORT
No 456 (R.A.A.F.) SQUADRON
R.A.F. Station, Ford, Sussex.

From:- R.A.F. Station, Ford, Sussex.   Serial AI/456/1 - 15/6/44.

To:- H.Q, A.D.G.B. (2 copies), H.Q, 11 Group (2 copies) O.C, R.A.A.F. O.C.
Ford, S.I.Os Tangmere, Bradwell Bay, Manston, Honiley, Hunsdon, Castle Camps,
Hurn, West Malling, H.Q, 100 Group, O.C. Durrington, I.O. 456 Squadron, file.

STATISTICAL

Date	(A)	15th June 1944
Unit	(B)	456 (R.A.A.F.) Squadron
Type and mark of our aircraft	(C)	1 Mosquito XVII; AI Mk X.
Time attack was delivered	(D)	0041
Place of attack	(E)	E. 59 (West of Beaumont Hague)
Weather	(F)	No cloud; clear; dark
Our casualties - aircraft	(G)	Nil
Our casualties - personnel	(H)	Nil
Enemy casualties in air combat	(J)	1 Ju 88 destroyed
Enemy casualties - ground or sea targets	(K)	Nil

GENERAL REPORT

Flight Lieutenant R.B.Cowper, D.F.C, (R.A.A.F.)(Pilot) and
Flying Officer W.Watson (R.A.F.)(Observer) were airborne from Ford at 2359
and landed 0250. They were vectord south by Black Gang. About twenty
minutes after take-off large flares were seen dropping over the sea at
about 3000 ft so they proceeded to investigate. A blip was picked up at
40 deg. above and to starboard, some six miles away. Pilot reported this
and was instructed by Control to investigate with extreme caution. Followed
target and obtained visual 10 deg. above and 1500 ft range on a Ju 88. It
was recognised by the shape of the wings and tail unit; engine exhausts
were also visible; it had a bola underneath and was not dropping Window.

F/Lt Cowper fired a 1½ seconds burst. The port motor of the
Ju 88 disintegrated; three of the crew were seen to bale out and a piece
of the e/a flew back and struck the starboard propeller spinner, denting it.
E/a dived to port in a spin and went straight down with flashes coming from
it. There was a big flash (quickly extinguished) as it hit the sea. Mosquito
was fixed by Black Gang at 0041 (Z.5613) after combat on the way home.
C.C.G. automatically exposed (1 ft film).

CLAIM   1 Ju 88 destroyed.

AMMUNITION (20 mm cannon: no stoppages)

	P.O.	P.I.	S.I.	S.O.	
HE/I	10	10	10	10	Total:
SAP/I	10	10	10	10	80 rounds.

R.B.Cowper F/Lt.   W.Watson   J.Armstrong
Flight Lieutenant   Flying Officer   Flying Officer
(Pilot)   (Observer)   (Intelligence Officer)

No 456 (R.A.A.F.) Squadron, R.A.F., Ford, Sussex.

Above and above right: Five nights later, on 15 June 1944, F/L Bob Cowper and F/L Bill Watson (above left) shot down a Ju 88 west of Beaumont Hague. The painting titled 'Chasing Shadows' by Barry Spicer captures the moment when some of the Luftwaffe crew baled out. (Courtesy © Barry Spicer, www.barryspicer.com)

2-second burst set his starboard wing ablaze. This wing burned heartily with huge flames and we flew parallel to e/a and slightly above to observe the finish. However, e/a released flaming object and it was seen that the starboard glider bomb had been ignited and was now flying solo, parallel to and between e/a and us. We immediately closed in to the attack again, and saw that the starboard wing of e/a was still burning outboard of engine nacelle. At this juncture e/a dived almost vertically towards the French Coast, W. of Cherbourg and following him down we fired a short burst into his rear. No additional effects were noticed. At 300ft we pulled out of the dive and e/a was still beneath us and just crossing the coastline. Visual was lost owing to the pilot having to give his whole attention to instruments in view of the dangerously low height.

'Pilot made a climbing turn to starboard and another contact was immediately obtained at approx 0405 head-on, slightly starboard, at 4000ft and 5 miles range. This a/c also was dropping Window. We continued to climb, and turning port, came in behind, and about 10 deg below, and obtained visual on a Do 217 at 2000ft. E/a was recognised by square outlines of twin tail unit, bulbous nose and broad rounded wings. He was carrying one glider bomb outboard of port nacelle but there was nothing visible under the starboard wing. No exhaust glow was visible and e/a took no evasive action, although continuing to drop Window. His speed was estimated at 240. One short burst was fired from 450ft which set the port engine and inboard mainplane ablaze. We took up position above and to port of e/a and watched the fire develop. E/a went into a steep diving turn to port, burning pieces falling off meanwhile; eventually it hit the beach, a ball of fire, and a brief interval later exploded, lighting up the whole area. No return fire had been experienced.

'Owing to the fact that the second contact was obtained immediately after breaking off the first engagement, the opportunity of observing the end of the *first aircraft was lost. However, when the second e/a blew up O, F/O Watson saw a large red fire inland from the coast in the direction that the first e/a had disappeared.'* [2]

Eight days after D-Day, on 13 June 1944, Germany launched its last major air offensive against the UK: the V1 campaign – or *Vergeltungswaffe* 1 (Revenge Weapon 1). These small, pilotless, pulse jet-powered flying bombs were launched from France against London and the south-east of England, day and night. Alongside their day-fighting cousins, night-fighting Mosquitoes were assigned to the anti-V1 campaign or anti-'Diver' patrols as they became known. Knocking a V1 down was not easy, especially at night! Firstly the Mosquito had to get on course behind the V1 (often having dived down to gain speed), then close for the attack and lastly be within range before the V1 reached the gun belt at the coast, or between this and the balloon belt south of London. Bob Cowper remembered these night interceptions:

'The Mosquito didn't have the speed to effect a normal interception of the V1. Many pilots developed their own methods of attacking them. The V1s generally came over the Channel at about one thousand feet above the water. Our method was to take the Mosquito to around six thousand feet and attempt to establish an imaginary interception point which would coincide with our aircraft's maximum speed in a dive. There were many moments during such an action when we would lose sight of the target and had to rely entirely on our original calculation, hoping, after being blind-spotted, to pick up the exhaust of the rocket. Sometimes we missed the interception point by arriving too early and at other times we were too late. In both circumstances, pulling the Mosquito out of a relatively steep dive at a speed well in excess of the manufacturer's recommendations was more important than any attempt to compensate for our misjudgement.'

Often the V1 blew up with great violence when hit by cannon and machine gun fire, causing damage to the attacking Mosquitoes,

---

[2]. The Heinkel was most likely He 177 A-5, W.Nr. 550175, F8+JH, from 1./KG 40, based out of Orleans-Bricy. During the engagement the pilot ordered the crew to bale out once the starboard wing was ablaze and two crew were taken prisoner, the radio operator and the rear gunner. The Do 217 probably came from KG 100.

often taking the form of the external fabric covering being burnt off, leaving a very singed aircraft. Mosquito crews soon learned that flying across the 'bows' of the V1 was enough to upset its simple guidance system, causing the V1 to dive into the Channel or open country and explode. This was known as a 'soft kill'. With the Allied ground offensive in Western Europe slowly but inexorably pushing the Germans back, they were forced to abandon their V1 launching sites in France around the Pas de Calais and instead devise the desperate plan of air-launching V1s against the UK from Heinkel He 111 H-22s (modified H-6/H-16 and H-21s) at dusk. The Heinkels flew very low over the North Sea to avoid radar and climbed to around 1,500 ft, firing off their V1s about 50 miles off the English coast before diving back down to almost wave-top height and scuttling back to their bases, initially located in Holland and later in Germany. The Heinkels came from III./KG 3 which, in time, became I./KG 53, soon

Right: W/C Hampshire and F/O Condon of 456 Squadron look at a flare pistol from the wreckage of a Ju 88 from KG 6, 3E+AP, which they shot down on the night of 24 March 1944 near Ford aerodrome. They were flying their usual NF. XVII, HK287 which was equipped with A.I. Mk. X (SCR 720) radar. 456 Squadron was one of the first units to receive this radar. A number of NF. XVIIs operated by 456 Squadron and other units were converted T. IIIs – the conversions being undertaken by Marshalls of Cambridge. (via David Vincent)

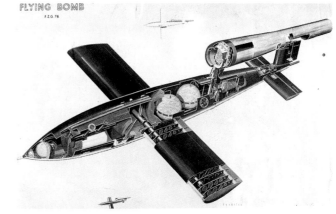

Wartime cut-away illustration of a V1. The flying-bomb campaign against England opened on 13 June 1944, eight days after D-Day. (U.S. Air Force)

A Heinkel He 111 of KG 53, showing the V1 attached to the lower starboard wing. These He 111s proved to be a difficult victory for Mosquito crews as they came in very low over the sea at dusk, creating hazardous interceptions due to poor light, slow interception speeds and proximity to the sea.

A V1 at the point of release from a He 111.

to be joined by II./KG 53 and III./KG 53. Attacking these low and slow-flying Heinkels, often in very poor weather and at dusk called for the utmost skill in flying by the Mosquito crews, which often frequently had to engage at near-stalling speed and very close to the sea. If they overshot the Heinkel they risked being fired at by the dorsal gunner at almost point-blank range (some of these later marks of He 111s used a heavy calibre MG 131 machine gun in the dorsal position). It was not without additional hazard, as Bob Cowper related regarding new crews joining the squadron: *'Their enthusiasm needed curbing with a reminder of the danger and difficulty of attempting to shoot down the Heinkels. Sergeant Mulhall was one of the new guys, an indefatigable, brash young Australian who wanted to shoot down any German aircraft still flying. He probably saw the low-flying Heinkels as easy prey but part of my job was to put a caution on such attempts. I would lecture them on the inherent danger of being over confident because catching these things was not only difficult, it was extremely exacting and dangerous as well. The Mosquito, with fifteen degrees of flap down, would be almost stalling and you were only feet above the sea. Sometimes you'd swear the spray from the waves was clouding the windscreen. There was more discomfort for the pilot when he flew the Mosquito below forty feet for at that point, a radio altimeter would*

engage a piercing horn and a bright red light would begin flashing, to remind him that he was flying dangerously low.'

Sadly for Sgt Mulhall, Cowper's advice was to no avail. He was to lose his life the following night when he flew into the Channel.

Not all of these engagements against the V1 carrying Heinkel's were to end badly for the Mosquito crews. FO Stevens and FO Kellet from 456 Squadron were up from Ford in their A.I. Mk. X-equipped NF. XVII on the night of 25 November 1944. The General Report states, *'They were patrolling under Frogspawn 2 (Bawdsey) at 2,500ft and seeing F/B's on a westerly course reported these and were given a Northerly vector. They had just turned on this course when three – four bright flashes, (air launched V1s) were seen off the starboard wing about 1,000ft below, coinciding with Frogspawn reporting a bogey to the East. The pilot turned starboard and dived to 1,500ft and at 04.45 observer obtained two contacts to port, both about two miles range. The nearest of these was chosen and it appeared to be flying in a easterly direction and taking evasive action. Mosquito went down to 500ft in pursuit. Control was told that this was being investigated but the message was apparently not heard owing to the fighter being too low. Target settled down on a mean track of 060 degrees at 500ft, with the Mosquito astern, and was weaving continuously never less than 30 degrees on either side, at the same time altering height. Closing very slowly (due to the fact that the C-scope was u/s) a visual was obtained at 800ft range but shortly afterwards lost before recognition could be affected owing to the target making a violent starboard turn. Mosquito made a half-*

orbit and contact was immediately regained, and after 10 minutes the target was seen again; there was no cloud but it was very dark. At 800ft range the target opened fire twice but did not hit the fighter, and at 600ft range (at a height of 900ft) it was identified as a He 111 by its various characteristic features.

'*At 600ft range pilot opened fire with a two-second burst. The e/a's port engine immediately caught fire, and closing in to 500ft, another two-second burst was fired, this appearing to go right through the fuselage. In the light of the flames the fin and rudder were noticed as being of a peculiar dull light grey camouflage. The Mosquito broke away to starboard, very close to the enemy aircraft, which could be seen to be going down in a gentle dive, flames from the port engine spreading. E/A hit the water and the wreckage bounced over the surface leaving a sea of flame. As the enemy aircraft went down after the attack it was noticed that a dozen or so green incandescent balls of no particular brilliance trailed out from it before it hit the sea. There was no Window. Claim: 1 He 111 destroyed.*'

The air–launched V1 campaign was soon to falter with the KG 53 suffering high losses. The last Heinkel to be shot down was on 6 January 1945. KG 53 ceased launch operations soon after having lost 77 Heinkels, 16 of these claimed by Mosquitoes.

The final night–fighter variant to see RAF service, the NF. 36 (a development of the NF. 30), was introduced too late to see combat in World War Two, but went on to see service in the RAF and foreign air forces well into the 1950s (see Chapter Nine). The final variant built was the NF. 38 with Merlin 114 engines, but none saw RAF service, most being sold to Yugoslavia. A minor point concerning the NF. 38 was that the cockpit canopy was increased in height by three inches and the windscreen was moved forward by five inches to create more room in the cockpit.

Many will say the Mosquito night–fighter, alongside the FB. VI, was de Havilland's finest use of the basic design. Its offensive role in countering the night Blitzes and intruder role over the Continent, not to mention its support and protection to Bomber Command aircraft, no doubt helped in severely denting the *Nachtjagdwaffe's* ability to wage its aerial campaign against the RAF heavies in the night skies over Germany.

Two views of 456 Squadron NF. XXXs at Bradwell Bay. These were the last Mosquito marks to see service with the Squadron and were powered by two-stage Merlin 72 or 76s, which gave a very useful boost in performance. They could reach a maximum speed of 424 mph at 26,000 ft. and proved to be an excellent night-fighter, coupled with the A.I. Mk. X (SCR 720) and continued in service with the RAF post-war. Bob Cowper is second from left in the photograph at left. (Bob Cowper)

The final night-fighter variant to see service with the RAF was the NF. 36, using A.I. Mk. X (SCR 720). Seen here is NF. 36, RL140, post-war in 199 Squadron colours. The squadron saw wartime use as a Radio Counter-Measures (RCM) unit between 1944-45. It was re-formed in July 1951 with Avro Lincolns (one of which can be seen in the background) as a unit of No. 90 Signals Group based at Watton and later Hemswell. It continued with RCM and was issued with some NF. 36s – these Mosquitoes saw service to 1953. RL140 was scrapped in 1955.

Mosquito NF. 36, RL140, 199 Squadron (No. 90 Signals Group) Hemswell, early 1950s

Ground crew of 29 Squadron conduct a dusk test-firing of an FB. VI's four .303 machine guns and four 20 mm cannon at Hunsdon – graphically showing the concentration of its armament. The FB. VI was to become the most numerous of Mosquito variants with production in the region of 2,700. It went on to to fulfil a host of offensive roles – from military transport,

GESTAPO-BUSTERS 8

The Fighter-Bomber FB.VI and the 2nd TAF

THERE is no doubting the destructive ability that the Mosquito FB. VI fighter-bomber had when it came on operations via the F. Mk. II version in May 1943. Built in more numbers than any other variant, around 2,700, RAF FB.VI squadrons were to wreak a path of destruction as they swept low and fast over Reich territory in the intruder and ranger role, day and night, to the war's end. Additionally in the Far East, FB.VIs operated from bases in India and Burma, taking the war to the Japanese alongside RAAF operated Mosquito fighter-bombers (in a limited role) in the South West Pacific area.

The seed for the Mosquito fighter-bomber was sown as early as July 1940 when thoughts turned to a fighter and night-fighter version. By December 1940 this had developed into a long-range convoy escort fighter and by 1941 with 'Intruding' in vogue, thoughts turned to F. IIs (NF. IIs shorn of radar) in offensive sweeps, carrying bombs. It should be noted that F. IIs gave long service in the day and night long-range intruder work (alongside NF. IIs and FB.VIs) well into January 1944.

Originally the FB. VI Series i could carry two 250 lb bombs in the rear of the bomb bay behind the cannon breaches. Later it was found that by clipping the bomb vanes on the 500 lb bomb these could replace the 250 lb bomb, thus doubling the load in the bomb bay; this modification and others were found in the Series ii. In addition two 250 lb (or two 500 lb) bombs could be carried under the wings or, alternatively, underwing drop tanks, rocket projectiles or depth charges could be carried. Combined with the existing cannon and machine guns, the FB. VI certainly packed a punch against enemy ground and shipping targets.

It did not stop there. In another development, the FB. XVIII had its four cannon replaced by a six-pounder 57 mm cannon primarily for use against U-boats and any unfortunate *Luftwaffe* aircraft that got in its way. That is not to say the fighter-bomber had it easy – Flak was undoubtedly

the greatest threat on these low-level operations and it became an increasing hazard as the war developed. Mother Nature also provided its own hazards, not least in the form of bird strikes.

The first true fighter-bomber was a conversion of a bomber B. IV airframe, DZ434, which embarked on its maiden flight on 1 June 1942 and 12 days later was delivered to Boscombe Down for evaluation as HJ661/G. With added armour plate across the front of the cockpit and later with Merlin 25 engines to improve low- and medium-level performance, de Havilland and its Mosquito had certainly come some distance from its unarmed philosophy. The first offensive attacks by 'fighter-bomber' units began in 1942 using Fighter F. IIs, but by May 1943 dedicated FB.VIs were coming off the production line in numbers and 418 (Intruder) Squadron RCAF was the first to use them on 7 May at Ford. Soon the type was serving with 25, 151, 157, 307, 410, 456 and 605 Squadrons, the score opening with a Ju 88 being shot down into the sea and three more damaged on 11 June. Depending upon unit role, these and subsequent squadrons were specialising in all manner of offensive work, military transport, communications, train-busting, bomber escort and airfield attacks, as well as shipping strikes.

Synonymous with the FB.VI was its role within the 2nd Tactical Air Force, a unit formed in June 1943 under the capable leadership

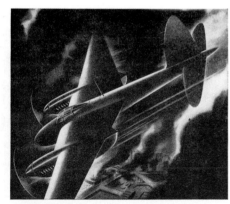

of AVM Basil Embry as a means of preparing 2 Group for invasion support in the run-up to Operation Overlord: the invasion of France. 464 (RAAF) and 487 (RNZAF) formed the initial 2nd TAF, joined soon after by 21 Squadron (all three squadrons jointly became 140 Wing) otherwise known as the Sculthorpe Wing. By early 1944, there were six squadrons within 2 Group and they mainly specialised in 'Noball' attacks against V1 launching sites in northern France, a dangerous task due to Flak defences and difficulty in identifying the sites. After D-Day, close tactical support to the Army became the 2nd TAF's prime objective and in the FB.VI it had the best means of achieving this due to its all-round capability.

But it was the 2nd TAF's low-altitude precision raids on the Gestapo in 1944-45 that were to make it famous back home and lift the spirits of those under Nazi rule.

The Amiens Prison raid

Just north of the town of Amiens on the main Amiens to Albert road stood a large prison. On 18 February 1944 its thick walls resounded to the din of attacking 2nd TAF Mosquitoes. The reason for this attack was a plea from the Resistance movement in France regarding the imminent execution of imprisoned Resistance members. Many had been arrested since December by a Gestapo crackdown through a suspected informer and much damage was being done to operations by the *Maquis* in the Somme area. Could the RAF bomb the prison to facilitate escape? The prison held around 712 captives of which some 200 were political prisoners and 120/180 were resistance agents. Basil Embry heard of the request and was keen to assist, just as the *Maquis* had assisted him when he was a prisoner of the Germans in 1940, although he was worried by the inevitable casualties of the bombing: '...*the idea of killing our own friends weighed heavily on my mind; it was a hateful responsibility.*'[1]

Nevertheless the operation went ahead. The attack called for the utmost planning and timing for the three squadrons taking part, with three waves of six Mosquitoes involved. 487 Squadron was tasked with breaching the outer prison walls in at least two places, with another wave from 464 Squadron tasked to hit prison buildings and guards' barracks. A third wave, from 21 Squadron, would be on standby to assist if the earlier attacks failed. The venerable G/C Percy Pickard was to lead the raid, flying in the second wave of 464 Squadron but in a 487 Squadron Mosquito, EG-F, HX922, to observe the results and call in 21 Squadron if he felt the need. The raid was planned for the 17th, but poor weather precluded and it was

postponed for 24 hours. The weather did not improve and a message from the Resistance warning: '*Strike now or never. The executions are imminent,*' galvanised action and the 18th was set.

After a detailed briefing, which involved a scale model of the prison and environs, the raiders took off in snowy weather from Hunsdon from where they were to link up with an escort of 22 Hawker Typhoons near the coast. At zero feet in now clear weather they raced across the Channel and crossed the French coast at 50 feet aiming for Tocqueville to bring them around to the north of Amiens. Using the long straight road from Albert to Amiens they made their attack at midday. A 487 Squadron pilot, P/O Max Sparks flying in EG-T, HX982, remarked in the first wave: '*We picked up the straight road from Albert to Amiens, and that led us to the prison. I shall never forget that road – long and straight and covered in snow. It was lined with tall poplars and the three of us were flying so low that I had to keep my aircraft tilted at an angle to avoid hitting the tops of the trees with my wing... The poplars suddenly petered out and there, a mile ahead, was the prison. It looked just like the briefing model and we were almost on top of it within a few seconds. We hugged the ground as low as we could, and at the lowest possible speed we pitched our bombs towards the base of the wall, fairly scraped over it – and our part of the job was over.*'[2]

In the second wave, Wg Cdr Bob Iredale of 464 Squadron recalled: '*...Clouds of smoke and dust came up, but over the top I could still see the triangular gable of the prison – my aiming point... I released my bombs from ten feet and pulled up slap through the smoke over the prison roof. I looked around to the right and felt mighty relieved to see the other boys still two hundred yards short of the target and coming in dead on line.*'[3]

Central to the leadership of the 2nd TAF was the straight talking and highly respected AVM Basil Embry, seen here (centre) in Copenhagen in July 1945. It was Embry who played a central role in 140 Wing's precision attacks on the Gestapo. He is flanked to his right by W/C Bob Iredale and G/C Bob Bateson, both of 464 Squadron, 2nd TAF. (via David Vincent)

1. *Strike Hard, Strike Sure: Epic of the Bombers,* Ralph Baker, Chatto & Windus, London 1963.
2, 3. *The Gestapo Hunters, 464 Squadron RAAF, 1942-45,* Mark Lax and Leon Kane-Maguire, Banner Books, Queensland, 1999.

4. Second section of second wave, **464 Sqn.**

Group Captain Pickard,
flew a 487 Sqn.
Mosquito, 'EG-F', HX922
in the last wave of
464 Sqn. Mosquitoes.

2. Second section of first wave, **487 Sqn.**

Only two Mosquitoes in 487s
second wave bombed the prison –
the third and lead machine 'EG-H'
suffering an engine fire en-route.

Holes breached in walls

Main strikes on prison

1. First section of first wave, **487 Sqn.**

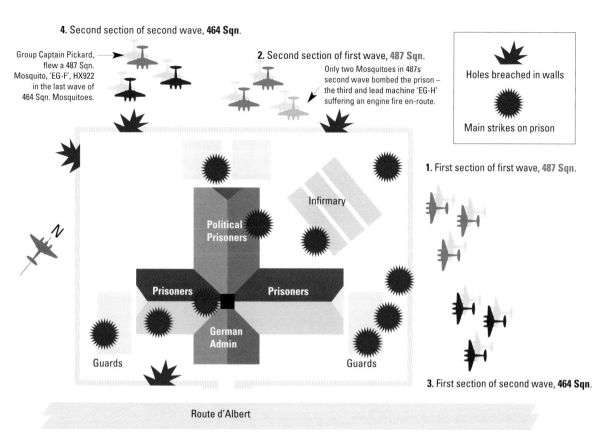

Infirmary

Political
Prisoners

Prisoners   Prisoners

German
Admin

Guards   Guards

3. First section of second wave, **464 Sqn.**

Route d'Albert

Above: Plan of Amiens prison showing the consecutive waves of 487 and 464 Squadron Mosquito fighter-bombers from 2nd TAF on their strike of 18 February 1944. Below and below left opposite page: Hunsdon in Hertfordshire was the base for the various Mosquito wings that took part in the prison raid and others. A memorial on the still active airfield (Microlight flying) commemorates all who served there between 1941-1945. (Stephen Skinner)

Top left and above: Two photographs of the Amiens jail-break in operation: the photograph above left shows the attack on the east wall and the above shows a fresh breach in the north wall.

Left: The well known and much liked G/C Percy Pickard, with his dog 'Ming'. Pickard with his navigator 'Bill' Broadley led the Amiens Prison raid flying a 487 Squadron Mosquito, 'EG-F', HX922. Sadly they were to loose their lives in the vicinity of the prison after being shot down by two Fw 190s of II./JG 26.

A number of holes were punched through the west and northern walls and the prison itself. Amid the dust and confusion, with concussion blowing open prison doors, prisoners made their escape to the waiting resistance outside in the surrounding countryside, though some lay wounded and dead along with many German guards whose barracks had been successfully targeted by the second wave. When the second wave had passed, Pickard, gratified by the raid's success, transmitted a code informing 21 Squadron that they were not required. Soon after, two Fw 190s of II./JG 26 bounced him at low level and, with his aircraft's tail severed by cannon fire, he and his long-time navigator 'Bill' Broadley died in the ensuing crash – a sad loss. The only other Mosquito loss was from 464 Squadron, SB-T, MM404, flown by S/L McRitchie and his navigator F/L R. W. Simpson who were hit by light Flak which killed Simpson; while a badly wounded McRitchie made a skilful crash-landing

and became a POW. Three other Mosquitoes were damaged and two Typhoons lost.

There has been debate regarding the success of the attack and the loss of life involved but 258 of the 712 escaped, some of whom were awaiting execution. The bombing and remaining German guards killed and injured around 180 prisoners and some were recaptured. Intriguingly, recent new information points to the raid being a ruse, part of an elaborate Allied intelligence operation to deceive the Germans as to the location of the forthcoming Allied invasion. What ever the true merits of the raid, not in doubt are two points: the success of the Mosquito in this role and the crews who flew them, and the bravery of the French Resistance, who were waging a war under very trying conditions against a very belligerent occupier – the *Wehrmacht* and the Gestapo. Amongst all this, the Resistance never failed to assist downed RAF crew – a debt the RAF owed. Five days

Left: A hole blown in the wall near the main entrance on the Route d'Albert. This wall was not targeted so the breach may have been caused by a ricocheting bomb.

Above: FB. VI, SB-V, MM403 of 464 Squadron, 140 Wing. Photographed in August 1944, when flown by F/O Roy Johnston and F/O Clive Turner. This Mosquito was a veteran of the Amiens prison raid, flown then by F/L McPhee and F/L Atkins. This Mosquito was abandoned by its crew on an intruder mission near Merville on 18 January 1945, when and engine cut and it lost height. (via David Vincent)

FB. VI, EG-T, MM417, photographed on 28 February 1944, was a Mosquito of 487 Squadron RNZAF, 140 Wing, 2nd TAF, one of the units that took part in the Amiens jail-break and many other precision raids thereafter. 'EG-T' flew in the prison raid, but not this Mosquito. The original 'EG-T', HX982 was damaged in the raid and replaced by MM417, whose operational life was cut short, when she was accidently shot at and severely damaged on 26 March 1944 during an attack on a V1 launch site by another Mosquito from the unit. MM417 made it back to Hunsdon to crash-land.

after the attack, the following message was received from a member of the *Maquis*: 'I thank you in the name of my comrades for bombardment of the prison. The delay was too short and we were not able to save all, but thanks to the admirable precision of attack the first bombs blew in nearly all doors and many prisoners escaped with help of the civilian population. Twelve of these prisoners were to have been shot the next day... .' (Even this

Far right: One of the attacking Mosquitoes over the shattered ruins of College Building No 4 at Aarhus University on 31 October 1944. Colleges 4 and 5 were completely destroyed, with College 5, the main building and barracks being severely damaged. The Aarhus attack was a complete success with more than 200 Gestapo and SD personnel killed and copious records destroyed. (via David Vincent)

A near life-size photograph of a 20 mm cannon shell as used by Mosquitoes. (Stephen Lewis)

message from the *Marquis* has been caught up in the 'ruse' theory, having purportedly not come from France, but from Whitehall!). Lastly an Australian navigator said of the attack, *'This was the sort of operation that gave you the feeling that if you did nothing else in the war, you had done something.'* [4]

These precision low-level attacks against the Gestapo were not to stop here. On 11 April 1944, they struck the Dutch Central Population Registry in the Hague, a building housing the Gestapo's records on the Dutch Resistance. The five-storey building collapsed. Four months later, on 14 July, Mosquitoes from 487 and 464 Squadrons delivered nine tons of bombs on the Gestapo barracks at Bonneuil Matours in shallow dives – and on it continued. On 1 August, 487 and 21 Squadrons using 24 Mosquitoes struck the SS barracks at Poitiers and on the following day 23 Mosquitoes attacked the sabotage school at Chateau Maulny. AVM Basil Embry led 14 Mosquitoes on 18 August to strike a school building at Egletons, used as SS barracks, destroying the target.

Aarhus University

Situated on the eastern side of the Jutland Peninsula in Denmark is a town called Aarhus, which housed the Aarhus University. During the war the Gestapo and the Secret Field Police HQ used three of these buildings for their nefarious activities. Records were kept on the Danish Resistance and interrogations were conducted. Additionally it was the centre for organising Danish informers. By mid–October 1944 the Danish Resistance requested help to suppress the Gestapo and its activities, particularly to destroy records, kill as many Gestapo personnel as possible and free prisoners. And so it was to be. On 31 October, 140 Wing led by Grp Capt Peter Wykeham-Barnes took 25 Mosquitoes escorted by 12 Mustangs from 306 Squadron to attack the Aarhus University. Stationed by this stage at Thorney Island, they flew to Swanton Morley where they picked up their escort for the 1,200 mile round trip – a good stretch of which would be over the North Sea. At 1140 hours they made their approach.

Sqd Ldr Ern Dunkley flying in SB-D, NS896 recalled: *'The University of Aarhus consisted of four or five buildings just next to an autobahn which ran ten miles in a straight line up to the place… The blokes who went in first had a good picture of the target, whereas those that followed had dust and smoke obscuring it…'* [5]

WC Langton in SB-F, NS994 recalled later in a BBC War Report, *'We headed towards the dust and smoke kicked up by our predecessors – we were the last to go in… I approached the target in a gentle curve and then*

dived onto the buildings. Fortunately we dropped our bombs slightly higher than we intended; I say fortunately because as it was, we felt the blast of some of the preceding bombs. As soon as we bombed, I pulled away in a climbing turn and as I did so I got a clear, if somewhat fleeting, glimpse of what remained of those buildings-just a couple of walls and debris flying all over the place… It was equally satisfactory to see bits of paper floating about at the height of our aircraft. As we turned away, Flak started coming up and we got a small hole in the wing but we got away with it, and the boys had destroyed a Gestapo Headquarters and what's more, we had helped the Danes.' [6]

The attack was a great success. The buildings were destroyed, leaving a hospital nearby unscathed. Between 150 and 160 Germans and around 30 collaborating Danes were killed, along with SS-*Obersturmführer* Lonechum, Head of the Security Services.

4. *Mosquito*, C. Martin Sharp and Michael J. F. Bowyer, Faber and Faber Ltd. London, 1967.
5. *Mosquito Monograph*, David Vincent, South Australia, 1982.
6. *The Gestapo Hunters, 464 Squadron RAAF, 1942-45*, Mark Lax and Leon Kane-Maguire, Banner Books, Queensland, 1999.

All of the Gestapo records were destroyed. Unfortunately around 10 civilians were killed but there were some astonishing escapes. Two prisoners were pulled alive from the ruins by friendly Danes, one of whom was being tortured by the Gestapo as the raid commenced. They died – he lived! It was an extremely successful operation with all aircraft returning safely, one landing in Sweden, the crew soon being repatriated.

Operation *Carthage*

The next operation, Operation *Carthage*, was mounted against the *Shellhus* (Shell House) building in Copenhagen, Denmark, HQ of the Gestapo. With news via the Resistance of impending executions on 21 March 1945, the raid was set for that date. The low-level experts of 140 Wing were tasked with the strike. They were now based at Amiens-Rosieres-en-Santerre in France, coincidentally just over a year since the Amiens prison raid. For this operation, however, they flew from an airfield in Norfolk to avoid overflying enemy territory and whilst there a Danish Resistance leader briefed them on the importance of the attack. Unfortunately this daring low-level raid, though successful, resulted in the deaths of 123 civilians including 86 children at the nearby *Jeanne d'Arc* convent school when one of the 20 Mosquitoes on the approach to the target collided with a 30 metre light stand and

crashed near the school. In the confusion, some of the following Mosquitoes bombed the now burning wreckage thinking it was the target and many bombs struck the school. However, eight 500 lb bombs did strike the *Shellhus*, six in the west wing, two in the east wing. The west wing collapsed under the weight of the bombs, a fire started and it effectively gutted the rest of the building. 56 Gestapo officials and Danish collaborators were killed along with eight

Far left top: The Shellhus is seen burning fiercely after the attack on 21 March 1945 during Operation Carthage. (via David Vincent)

Above: Two photographs taken from a rearward-facing camera from one of the attacking Mosquitoes as they exit Copenhagen after dropping their bombs on the Shellhus. In both photographs a second Mosquito, from 487 Squadron can be seen at very low level from following behind. (via David Vincent)

Left: The gutted Shellhus post-war. Though appearing intact, little remained behind the facades. Traces of its wartime camouflage applied by the Germans can be seen. Six Germans and 50 Danish collaborators were killed along with countless files and documents destroyed by the fire that raged after the bombs were dropped (some records state up to 200 German and Danish collaborators were killed). Out of the 26 prisoners in the building, 18 survived. The Shellhus was so badly damaged it was replaced with a new building in 1951. (via David Vincent)

No. 140 Wing 'Ops' board for 4/5 May 1945. Crews from 21 and 464 Squadrons were briefed for operations that night, but were stood down due to the unconditional surrender of the German forces. Note the comment chalked in under 'Remarks' – 'Cancelled due to unconditional surrender of enemy'. (via David Vinvcent)

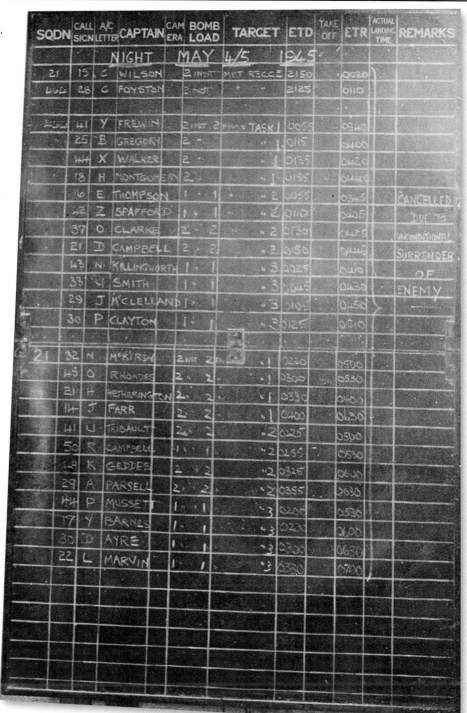

SQDN	CALL SIGN	A/C LETTER	CAPTAIN	CAMERA	BOMB LOAD	TARGET	ETD	TAKE OFF	ETR	ACTUAL LANDING TIME	REMARKS
			NIGHT	MAY	4/5	1945					
21	15	C	WILSON	2 INST		MET RECCE	2150		0020		
464	28	C	FOYSTON	2 INST			2125		0110		
464	41	Y	FREWIN	2 INST 2 FPS		TASK 1	0055		0340		
	25	B	GREGORY	2			0115		0400		
	44	X	WALKER	2		1	0135		0420		
	18	H	MONTGOMERY	2		1	0155		0440		
	16	E	THOMPSON	1	1	2	0055		0345		CANCELLED
	42	Z	SPAFFORD	1	1	2	0110		0405		DUE TO
	37	O	CLARKE	2	2	2	0130		0425		UNCONDITIONAL
	21	D	CAMPBELL	2	2	2	0150		0445		SURRENDER
	43	N	KILLINGWORTH	1	1	3	0025		0110		OF
	33	Y	SMITH	1	1	3	0045		0430		ENEMY
	29	J	MCCLELLAND	1		3	0105		0450		
	30	P	CLAYTON	1		3	0125		0510		
21	32	N	McKIRDY	2 INST 2 FPS		1	0230		0500		
	45	O	RHOADES	2	2	1	0300		0530		
	21	H	HETHERINGTON	2	2	1	0330		0600		
	14	S	FARR	2	2	1	0400		0630		
	41	U	THIBAULT	2		2	0235		0500		
	50	R	CAMPBELL	1		2	0255		0530		
	49	K	GEDDES	2	2	2	0325		0600		
	29	A	PARSELL	2	2	2	0355		0630		
	44	P	MUSSETT	1	1	3	0200		0530		
	17	Y	BARNES	1	1	3	0230		0600		
	30	D	AYRE	1	1	3	0300		0630		
	22	L	MARVIN	1	1	3	0330		0700		

prisoners, though some managed to escape. Copious records and documents were also destroyed which severely hindered Gestapo operations. Three other Mosquito crews were lost on the return leg due to damage, having to ditch in the sea off Zeeland, and two Mustangs of the escort were lost.

140 Wing felt the tragedy of the bombing of the *Jeanne d'Arc* school badly – the worst in all its months of operations – but the Danes forgave. The replacement *Shellhus* today is the head office of the Shell Oil Company (as it was pre-war) and, in honour of the RAF crews killed in the attack, there is a bronze cast of a propeller from one of the crashed Mosquitoes mounted on the building with the crews' names on a plaque below.

The final pinpoint Gestapo raid of the war was on the island of Fyn, north-west of Odense, on 17 April 1945, where the Gestapo had an HQ called 'Torture Castle' by the locals. Six Mosquitoes from 140 Wing escorted by eight Mustangs took off from Melsbroek and headed north towards the Jutland Peninsula and the island. The Gestapo had by now realised that camouflaging buildings well could aid their survival and this had the Mosquitoes and Mustangs milling about in the area for nearly half an hour. But the target was eventually identified and effectively destroyed, though ricocheting bombs hit some surrounding houses killing upwards of 14 people. It must be remembered that the RAF felt deeply about the civilian losses on these raids and, in a post-war ceremony at Aarhus, a considerable sum of money that had been collected throughout the RAF was handed over to the Crown Prince of Denmark.

Mosquito FB. VI, SB-Y, TA475 of 464 Squadron in July 1945. TA475 later passed to 107 Squadron and swung on landing, collapsing the undercarriage at Gutersloh in October 1946. (via David Vinvcent)

This page: The backbone of any squadron was the ground crews, as without their tireless efforts, in all weathers and at all times of day, none of the operations would have taken place. Seen here are some of the day-to-day tasks including the bombing up of 2nd TAF FB. VIs; the aircraft could take either a 250 lb or a 500 lb bomb under each wing and a further two in the rear of the bomb bay. On dark nights the bomb bay load was replaced by flares. (via David Vincent)

ROCKFIST ROGAN R·A·F

An Ace Story
Of an
Ace Air-Fighter

CHAPTER 1
Shot Down Over Germany

FLIGHT-LIEUTENANT ROGAN, of the R.A.F., better known as Rockfist because of his boxing record, leaned back against the mantelpiece in the ante-room of the officers' mess of the Freelance Squadron, chuckled and surveyed his pals.

Rockfist, Curly Hooper, Archie Streatham and a few more of the pilots of the famous fighter squadron were swopping yarns. The subject had got round to boxing, and Archie Streatham, the monocled dude of the squadron, was holding the floor.

"Do you chappies remember before the war when Rockfist took on that beastly big heavyweight from Germany?" he drawled. "Name

By Hal Wilton

of Franz Goulter. Must have weighed sixteen stone——"

"Coooooooooh !" said a wondering voice behind him.

Archie swung round and faced a pilot officer named Jack Jenkins, who had quite recently joined the Freelance Squadron. The disbelieving remark appeared to have come from him.

"There's no need to be rude," drawled Archie with great dignity. "If you don't believe me, ask Curly. He was there, acting as Rockfist's second. As I was saying," he went on, turning to the rest of his audience, "it was a pretty tough fight for the first five rounds. But then Rockfist got on top, and began to knock his man all round the ring. The sixteen-stone slogger didn't stand an earthly. Rockfist caught him a

79

Above: The precision low-level attacks conducted by various Mosquito squadrons led to much publicity in the UK and, in turn, influenced some boys' fiction post-war. 'F/L "Rockfist" Rogan' with Curly Hooper, and Archie Streatham, his fellow chums of the 'Freelance Squadron', were somewhat in the 'Biggles' mould and appeared in the 'Champion Annual for Boys' in 1947. As seen in the illustration above, Rogan has been able to lead, bomb and navigate at low level to the target in his Mosquito B. IV all by himself – quite a feat! 'An Ace Story of an Ace Air-fighter' if ever there was one. (via Michael Davies)

Below: Mosquito FB. VIs of 464 Squadron at Hunsdon, show clearly the wear and tear associated with their operations. Mosquito SB-Y, HX921, later served with the squadron as SB-P. (via David Vincent)

Above: Sgt Dean and F/S Ivo De Souza of 464 Squadron board their Mosquito for a night operation on 7 June 1944 at Gravesend. De Souza was one of a small number of West Indians to serve as aircrew during the war in England – and possibly the only one to serve on an RAAF unit. 464 Squadron was not entirely Australian: like many Commonwealth squadrons in the UK, it had many other nationalities serving within its ranks. Sgt Dean was RAF – from Middlesex. De Souza was very popular in the squadron and became a diplomat after the war. (via David Vincent)

FB. VI, *'Black Rufe'*, TH-M, NS850, 418 (Intruder) Squadron, RCAF

NS850 was a Hatfield-built Mosquito, flown by S/L Robert Allan Kipp DFC, DSO and F/L Peter Huletsky DFC and Bar. For the period 1943 to 1945, Kipp and Huletsky were to have much success – claiming 10 aircraft shot down and one shared destroyed, one shared probable, one damaged, seven destroyed on the ground and eight damaged on the ground. The bulk of the tally was scored in the seven months between December 1943 and June 1944. The Mosquito was written off in a landing accident at Hunsdon on 1 November 1944 following a single-engine landing.

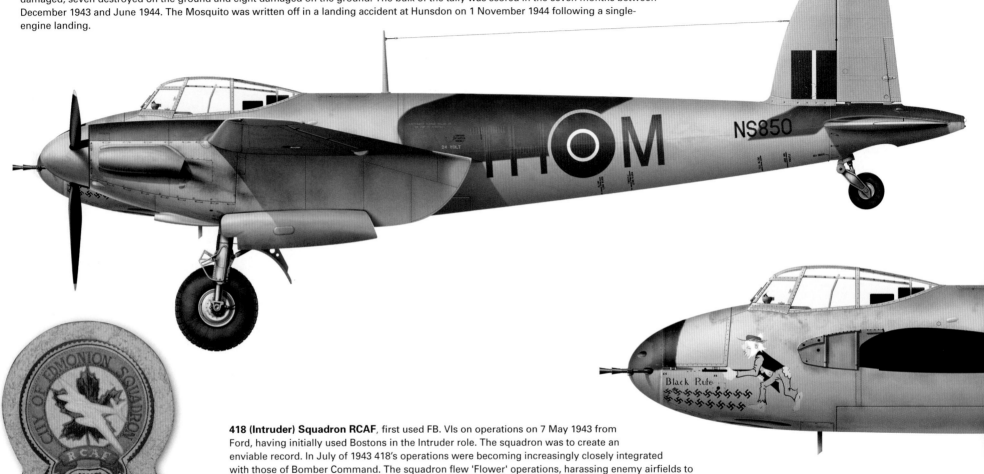

418 Squadron's unofficial crest. This example made out of wood and fabric was made during the war by a member of the squadrons ground crew and presented to John Howell, a navigator who flew with the squadron (see opposite page top). (John Howell)

418 (Intruder) Squadron RCAF, first used FB. VIs on operations on 7 May 1943 from Ford, having initially used Bostons in the Intruder role. The squadron was to create an enviable record. In July of 1943 418's operations were becoming increasingly closely integrated with those of Bomber Command. The squadron flew 'Flower' operations, harassing enemy airfields to suppress fighters while the bombers flew overhead, during the saturation raids on Hamburg and Berlin, as well as during the Milan-Turin series of raids. By August, 418 was, for the first time, attacking airfields within the borders of Germany itself. At the same time, the squadron was keeping the pressure up on Hitler's transportation systems, strafing trains and bombing railways, as well as the occasional naval vessel. It even participated in the 'Dambuster' raid on 16 September, providing fighter cover and close support for the Lancasters of 617 Squadron. In April/May of 1944 during a six-week period, the squadron destroyed 30 enemy aircraft in the air, plus four probables, and a further 38 destroyed on the ground and 20 damaged. At the end of 1944, 418 Squadron came under the jurisdiction of 136 Wing (2nd TAF), and no longer conducted its standard intruder role. Instead, it strafed convoys and barges, bombed railway junctions, and attacked enemy ground forces in support of the Allied armies. It performed this role during the 'Battle of the Bulge' in the Ardennes at the beginning of 1944, as well as during 'Operation Clarion' in February. The victory tally of 418 for the 37 months from its formation to the end of the war reads as follows: 3,492 sorties, for a total of 11,248 hours airborne, destroying 178 enemy aircraft, 105 of them in the air and 73 on the ground; another 103 damaged, and 9 'probable' kills. All of its airborne victories were achieved without the aid of Airborne Intercept radar, relying on visual contact alone. 83 V1 rockets fell to 418's Mosquitoes as well. (Sourced from the 418 Squadron Association website)

Left: Typical of some of the crews who flew Mosquitoes during the war were F/O F. M. Sawyer (far left) from Rossland, British Columbia and F/O John Howell from Northamptonshire in the UK. John Howell trained as a navigator in Canada where he joined up with 418 Squadron and its Mosquitoes (including Sawyer), after topping his course in navigation. In turn, John became 418's longest serving member at 16 months. They started their Mosquito time in Britain by making dummy Intruder training flights to Ireland and in March 1943 they arrived at Ford with 418 where they flew together until almost the end of the war, finishing it whilst based at Volkel (B80) in the Netherlands. John stayed in the RAF post-war, serving with several Mosquito squadrons in Germany and in the UK up to 1950 with a total of eight years on Mosquitoes. He emigrated to Australia with his wife in 1951, continuing a career in aviation with Qantas Airways. (John Howell)

Number of Flights (= number of take-offs & landings) during 1943-1950, flown by John Howell (Navigator) = 336

Location	Country	No of Flights
Greenwood (Nova Scotia)	Canada	23
High Ercall	UK	28
Ford	UK	12
Holmsley South	UK	78
Hurn	UK	9
Middle Wallop	UK	28
Hunsdon	UK	19
Hartford Bridge	UK	19
Coxyde	Belgium	23
Volkel	Holland	12
Gütersloh	Germany	35
Klagenfurt	Austria	3
Wahn	Germany	10
Gatow	Germany	2
Lübeck	Germany	17
Andover	UK	18

Total 336 (Covering all activities)
These included:

Operations: **59**

Night-flying tests (NFTs)

Specific test-flights

Practice flying

Detachment flights eg. Berlin, Lübeck, Austria – 'Cold War'

Moving base

Specific missions ('Torch')

Gunnery exercises

Specific training (Formation)

Bombing practice

Weather recon.

Search & Rescue

Air/air firing practice (drogue)

S/engine practice

Photo recon.

Low-level practice

418 Squadron members pose for a photograph in front of FB. VI, flown by F/O Sid Seid and his navigator F/O Dave McIntosh. Sid Seid was an American of Jewish descent and apparently would stop at nothing to get at the enemy. The emblem on the crew access door is 418's unofficial crest (as seen on opposite page. F/O John Howell is standing eighth from the right. (John Howell)

The Banff Strike Wing and the nearby Dallachy Strike Wing enjoyed spectacular success in anti-shipping role for the short period they were active. Between September 1944 and May 1945, the Banff Strike Wing was under the command of Group Captain The Hon. Max Aitken, son of the then Lord Beaverbrook. Operating a mixed force of Beaufighters and Mosquitoes out of Scotland, its six multinational squadrons took a heavy toll of German shipping carrying vital iron ore and other supplies, in concentrated attacks in the North Sea and along the Norwegian coastline. U-boats and Luftwaffe aircraft also came under the umbrella of operations. Often penetrating deep into heavily defended fjords to reach their anchored supply ship targets, the Strike Wing crews ran the gauntlet of formidable anti-aircraft fire. The wing was unique because of the presence of 333 Squadron, Royal Norwegian Air Force, which formed one of its component elements. The squadron's skills in the air and its ability to locate targets concealed in mountain-fringed fjords became one of the Banff Wings great strengths and helped the joint RAF, Norwegian and Commonwealth aircrews who made up the unit achieve outstanding success in the destruction of supply ships, Flak ships and U-boats. However, this was not without cost – more than 80 strike crews died on these operations. In the photograph here, 248 Squadron Mosquitoes are seen taxiing on a perimeter track. 17 Mosquitoes can be seen in the original photograph plus one Percival Proctor.

Mosquito FB. VI, NE-Y, of 143 Squadron, Banff Strike Wing, fully loaded with semi-armour-piercing rockets, low over the sea.

Below: 4 May 1945, Banff Strike Wing's final attack on shipping in the Kiel and Kattegat areas. The squadrons involved were 143, 235, 248, 333 and 404, led by Wing Commander Pierce, and consisting of forty-one Mosquitoes, eighteen Mustangs for fighter cover and three Air Sea Rescue Warwicks on hand to drop lifeboats to any ditched crews. A convoy was spotted consisting of an N-class minesweeper, three merchant vessels, one ex Dutch gunboat and two smaller enemy vessels. The German merchant vessel 'Wolfgang L.M. Russ' of 3750 tons was sunk and another German merchant vessel damaged, the 'Gunther Russ' of 998 tons. The Danish merchant vessel 'Angamos' of 3540 tons was also damaged. The Flak barrage was intense which resulted in four Mustangs failing to return. Two Mosquitoes suffered battle damage and landed in neutral territory. During the attack on the shipping near Samso Island all the vessels were 'seen to be hit' by either rocket projectiles or 20 mm cannon fire. One Mosquito landed back at Banff with the German ensign and part of the mast of a ship embedded in the nose of the aircraft, after colliding with it at low level. Later reports state that all ships were left either smoking or on fire. At least nine Mosquitoes can be seen in this photograph.(WW2 Images)

Above: On 2 April 1945, a large strike force from Banff consisting of Mosquitoes from 143, 235, 248 and 333 Squadrons, attacked shipping at Sandefjord, including a tanker in dry dock. Two vessels were sunk: the 'Concordia', a Norwegian merchant vessel of 5154 tons, and the German merchant vessel 'William Blumer' of 3604 tons. Another four ships were severely damaged: the German merchant 'Shios Espana' of 7465 tons and the 'Kattegat' of 6031 tons, the other ships being the Norwegian merchant vessels 'Hektor' of 5742 tons and 'Belpamela' of 3165 tons. This was a successful strike, but three Mosquitoes were lost. (WW2 Images)

Banff Strike Wing Mosquito FB. VI, NE-D, RS625 of 143 Squadron, benefiting from a later modification which allowed the carrying of 100 gallon drop tanks and multiple rockets at the same time. This aircraft also had an F.24 camera in the nose. This Mosquito, a late model Series ii, was from a batch built at Hatfield, most of which went to Coastal Command. RS625 was scrapped in November 1955. (via David Vincent)

Left: Mosquito FB. VIs of Royal Navy No. 811 Squadron, photographed in 1945/46. Mosquitoes from this unit took part in a victory flypast over London on 8 June 1946. Note that the armament on these FB. VIs has been restricted to the four 20 mm cannon. This unit also operated TR. 33s which were a post-war torpedo-reconnaissance fighter-bomber designed for carrier-borne use. The TR. 33 had a reinforced fuselage, arrestor hook, four-bladed propellers, manually-folding outboard wings and later models had redesigned undercarriage struts with smaller diameter wheels to reduce bounce on carrier landing.

Atmospheric photograph of Australia's first fighter-bomber A52-1, now camouflaged (see page 33). It shares a damp ramp after a thunderstorm with another twin-engine aircraft immediately in front of it – possibly a Beaufighter – and to the left is a prototype developmental airframe of the C.A.C. Boomerang fighter, the CA-14A, A46-1001, modified to have a square fin and rudder. (via David Vincent)

Above: FB. VI, A52-526, NA-E, (ex HR506), of No. 1 (Attack) Squadron RAAF, seen at Morotai (located in the Halmahera group of eastern Indonesia's Maluku Islands in the Dutch East Indies) on 18 March 1945. Spitfire Mk. VIIIs of No. 457 Squadron can be seen sharing the strip. This Spitfire squadron was known as the 'Grey Nurse Squadron', due to the aircraft having shark mouths painted on their cowlings. 457 Squadron was formed in the UK on 16 June 1941, and saw much action over France on fighter sweeps as part of No. 11 Group. The squadron was stood down in late May 1942, for redeployment to Northern Australia to counter Japanese air raids. Two other Spitfire squadrons from the UK, joined 457 – 452, another RAAF unit and No. 54 Squadron RAF. 457 went into action in March 1943. Mosquito A52-526 survived the war to be sold in 1950. (via David Vincent)

Left: FB. VIs of No. 1 (Attack) Squadron, No. 86 Wing, RAAF at Labuan Island, Borneo in August 1945. These fighter-bombers were British-built and NA-L, A52-508 was ex HR307. The majority of squadron aircraft participated in only one operation before the Japanese surrender in August 1945. Top scorer in the unit was A52-511, NA-G which flew four operations. By November all Mosquitoes had returned to Australia as the wet season in Borneo was causing deterioration of mainplane fabric and swelling of plywood. The squadron disbanded on 7 August 1946 at Narromine in NSW. (via David Vincent)

British-built FB. VIs supplemented Australian-built FB. Mk. 40s for RAAF operational use. This example appears as if it may be serving with No. 1 Squadron, it may very well be possibly a Mosquito called 'Pera Sayap', so titled by the squadron on the port side of the nose. Part of a serial can be seen A52-51 plus what appears to be a portion of the large black 'N', part of No. 1s fuselage code 'NA'. Note the bare metal Spitfire Mk. Vs in the background. (via David Vincent)

Reloading the four 20 mm cannons in an NF. 36 of No. 39 Squadron in Egypt. (Peter Verney)

Some very tight formation flying is seen here by three NF. 36s of 39 Squadron. These Mosquito night-fighters were the last of their breed in RAF service and carried the A.I. Mk. 10 (SCR 720) airborne radar, which first saw use during the war. It continued in use in the Meteor night-fighter, the NF. 13. (Peter Verney)

A POST-WAR REFLECTION 9

Peter Verney's Polish pilot, F/S Joe Halkiew, who had wartime experience on the Mosquito, sits in his 'office'. (Peter Verney)

Left: Joe Halkiew and Peter Verney stand in front of their NF. 36 of 39 Squadron. No. 39 Squadron re-formed in March 1949, flying Hawker Tempests in the fighter-bomber role based at Khartoum. In the same year it re-equipped with NF. 36s and became the only night-fighter unit in the Middle East, until No. 219 Squadron joined it in March 1951. Meteor NF. 13s replaced the Mosquitoes in November 1952. (Peter Verney)

Peter Verney, ex Navigator/Radar Operator

'I joined the RAF in July 1950 as a trainee navigator, and after ITS at Jurby on the Isle of Man, in December 1950 commenced navigation training at No. 1 ANS at Hullavington. By this time the Government had become concerned at the Russians' possession of nuclear weapons and the build up of their bomber force, based upon the Boeing B-29 copy that Tupolev was producing. As a result the Meteor NF. 11 was produced as an interim lash-up night-fighter and there was a rapid expansion of the night-fighter force in Fighter Command. In consequence extra crews were required and my course was transferred at the end of August 1951 from navigation training at the completion of the Basic stage to the Night-Fighter OCU, No. 228, at Leeming, before we had been awarded our wings and whilst we still held the rank of Officer Cadet. In normal circumstances we would have proceeded to the Advanced stage and spent a further five months or so training before being awarded the 'N' brevet and then going on to an OCU.

'Some 15 out of the 32 who had started the course at Jurby and completed the A.I. school in October were awarded a navigator/radio "N" flying badge. About half were commissioned as Pilot Officers and the rest promoted to Sergeant, which was the norm for the time. We then joined No. 2 Squadron of the OCU and were introduced to the bunch of pilots with whom we were to crew up to fly the Mosquito NF. 36. One of these was a Pole, F/S Joe Halkiew, who had wartime Mosquito experience and who several people wanted to fly with. Luckily he chose me and we subsequently had almost five successful years together.

'We had one dodgy incident at Leeming when we did our first high-level 25,000 feet night cross-country on the Mosquito, and which was about the first time I had used oxygen. When at about 45 minutes after take-off I turned to Joe and complained that I did not know how to use the Dalton navigational computer, he realised that I was suffering from lack of oxygen and found that we had in fact run out. He immediately descended to 10,000 feet and we carried on. I did not receive a very good mark for this exercise and it had to be

repeated. This course lasted about eight weeks with some 38 hours on the Mosquito and my log book records "…on *14 January 1952 Awarded Fighter Command Category 'C'*" as a Navigator/radio.

'Joe and I, in company with another NCO crew, were posted to Egypt and early in February 1952 we boarded an Avro York at Blackbushe for Fayid in the Suez Canal Zone. On arrival we were given transport to Kabrit, which was home to two night-fighter squadrons, 39 and 219, both equipped with the Mosquito NF. 36. It also housed 13 Squadron with the Mosquito PR. 34, though in the process of converting to the Meteor PR. 10, and 683 Squadron with Lancasters, which was doing an aerial survey of Africa and which soon departed.'

39 Squadron RAF Kabrit, Suez Canal Zone, Egypt

'When we arrived the situation in Egypt was total chaos, and because of the rioting which had occurred in Cairo the previous year and the subsequent attempts by the Egyptians to remove us from the Canal Zone, our forces had been doubled in strength. Unfortunately stores and food supplies did not keep pace and at times our rations were extremely short and often of poor quality. Beer and bread were only available on about three or four days a week. We were expected to carry a service revolver and 12 rounds of ammunition when flying but the stores had no holsters or ammo pouches so we were forced to carry our armament loose in our pockets! We had only been there a few weeks when there was the most almighty sandstorm which lasted about two days. When it was possible to resume work we found that our hangar doors would not close by about 400 mm at one end and the hangar was some 150 mm deep in sand. After the aircraft had been pushed out and brushed off someone had the bright idea of opening the hangar at each end, reversing the tail of a Mosquito in, and, by running up both engines, assist a line of men with brooms to sweep the floor. This worked a treat and created another sandstorm, much to the annoyance of the Wing Commander Flying, whose office roof had been blown off and whose clerks had almost finished straightening out his paperwork, and which bore the full blast. Our CO got a rather different one!

'Flying in Egypt was a new experience. We were sent off on cross-country flights which included traversing the Nile delta at high and low level by day. At night we had a cross-country which included a turning point at Neckl in the middle of the Sinai Desert. I found a few faint lights and concluded that I had missed the town shown on the map: later we had a look by day and found there were only a few scruffy buildings at a crossroads of desert tracks. Most of our flying took place over the Sinai, which was a strange landscape of shifting sand dunes in the North and barren rocky mountains to the South. Occasionally we would see a Bedouin walking along totally alone and miles from anywhere, or small groups with a cluster of black tents and small herds of goats or sheep. We came across one of these herds with a few Bedouin in attendance whilst low flying one day. I am ashamed to say we amused ourselves by flying low over them and stampeding them in the direction of some soft sand. There was a tank unit nearby and we would see them exercising in the desert. Joe found a new game in flying down the trail of sand thrown up by a fast moving tank, and zooming over the hapless commander standing up in the turret. Later on we had a visit from the officers of this unit, which caused considerable amusement in the crewroom. Nearly half the Squadron's aircrew were NCOs, and nearly all the Squadron's aircrew were sat around the crewroom playing cards or drinking tea when our CO brought in the tank CO to introduce us. We shambled to our feet as only aircrew can, as this officer appeared. When he realised that there were NCOs present – he apparently expected all aircrew to be commissioned, he stopped with a horrified look on his face, turned to our CO and said, "I suppose you have to take an NCO along to do the work", turned on his heel and hurried out. We were not so amused when some of the tank officers were given rides on air to ground firing sorties and most were airsick over our radar sets!'

Gunnery

'We soon settled into the standard night-fighter squadron routine of NFT's and ciné, with PI's (Practice Interceptions) under the control of local GCI (Ground Control Interception) radar. I should explain that ciné was an exercise using the gun camera, carrying out high quarter attacks, to give the pilots practice in deflection shooting. The Mosquito had a simple ring gunsight and so pilots had to learn the basic lead-off gunnery as one would use when firing a shotgun. To this end the camp had a clay pigeon range where our gunnery officer used to organise Saturday morning shoots. I used to help him by doing some of the ciné film assessing, i.e. running the film one frame at a time and measuring the range, the deflection allowed and angle off of the target, to assess the pilot's accuracy, and in return he would allow me to have a go at the clays. There was also a strong emphasis on air-to-ground firing which was carried out on a range at Shallufa. This range was on bare rocky desert and it was absolutely essential to turn sharply away from the line of fire when pulling out from the firing dive to avoid ricochets and lumps of rock. We did have an aircraft written off because a ricochet dented the laminated wooden main spar. If the main spar was damaged within 18 inches of an engine mounting, no repair was allowed and the aircraft was a write-off. During the day the local women and children could be seen running about under the aircraft as they were firing and picking up the 20 mm cartridge cases as they fell! At night it was even more entertaining as the navigators had to fly so that they could read off the altimeter and remind the pilot to begin the pull out from the dive at the specified 400 ft: this meant that recovery was often well below 300 ft. A pilot from 219 seriously frightened his navigator one night when he opened his throttles abruptly during this manoeuvre and the torque rolled the aircraft onto its back! He had the presence of mind to complete the roll and regain control.

'Firing the guns was an experience: the cockpit floor was a sheet of ply, immediately below which were the 4 x 20 mm cannon so that while the pilot's feet were raised on the rudder pedals, for the navigator it felt as though there was someone belting the floor beneath with a baulk of timber.'

Piloting the Mosquito

'We returned to a normal routine at Kabrit carrying out all the usual exercises, amongst which pilots were required to undertake two practice single-engine overshoots and one single-engine landing per month, so that they could cope when it really mattered. When on one engine the decision to land had to be made at 800 ft at night and 300 ft by day, as the aircraft had to be dived while the undercarriage and flaps were retracting so that a safe climbing speed could be attained. While the Mosquito could be safely flown on one engine, it would not maintain height above 5,000 ft, and full power was required which could soon lead to the live engine overheating. It was an endurance test for the pilot, as he had to keep the rudder held against the live engine. At the maximum speed under those conditions of about 155 knots it was fairly heavy, even with full rudder trim wound on, but the load increased as speed was reduced until, at about 137 knots, the pilot could no longer keep the aircraft straight and level. This so-called safety speed had to be determined whenever an engine was shut down, as losing control under these circumstances was one of the leading causes of Mosquito accidents. Incidentally, the advice if an engine failed on take-off and safety speed had not been attained was: put the aircraft down straight ahead. To attempt to turn led to the aircraft rolling over and diving in and many crews crashed in this way, I suppose it was a crash either way, but at least, as my roommate at Leeming proved, straight ahead one had a chance of getting away with it. He and his pilot had an engine go immediately at take-off. They went through the boundary hedge, across the road and out into the next field, losing pieces of aircraft as they went. Luckily the live prop was the starboard, it came off and travelled about 100 yards laterally. The port prop stood in the field like the proverbial blasted oak tree, but they got away with the obligatory bang on the head, and were none the worse after a night in sick quarters.

'The hazards of Mosquito flying were vividly demonstrated to me one day when I flew with one of the more exuberant pilots, who asked if I would like to see some aerobatics, which of course was strictly forbidden. Naturally I agreed and we flew a nice gentle barrel roll followed by a loop, which was very slow over the top, and then he decided to try a roll off the top. All went well until he pushed the stick over to roll out while inverted, then all hell broke loose with land and sky rapidly changing places several times while we banged our heads together at the top of the cockpit. Meanwhile the pilot, who could just reach the top of the stick, was vainly stirring it round until we entered a conventional spin, which seemed like a series of flick turns, from which he eventually recovered, and we very steadily and soberly returned to Kabrit. We concluded that we had managed about three or four turns of an inverted spin followed by the same of a normal spin, it certainly used up a lot of height, but we remained friends and I kept my mouth shut!

'Bomber Command Lincolns had a regular "Sunray" exercise to Shallufa and we normally did a night exercise with them. On one of these we intercepted a Lincoln and in accordance with the rules pulled up on his port side to claim the kill by flashing the navigation lights on and off. There was no response to several seconds flashing and Joe, who was an excellent formation flyer, became impatient and drew up close with our wingtip tucked well inside that of the Lincoln. Then he turned on the nav lights again and illuminated the Lincoln cockpit, that got a response all right and there were torches flashed at us from the length of the aircraft.

'We had been told that we were to be re-equipped in early 1953 with the Meteor NF. 13, which was an NF. 11 still equipped with

A.I. Mk.10 but with a radio compass and Rebecca/Babs electronic equipment fitted in lieu of the SCR 729 beacon system that our Mosquitoes carried, also a refrigeration unit to civilise the cockpit. Incidentally Mosquito cockpit temperatures could reach 160°F (70°C), and we had a nasty experience while night flying after having done 3 hours low level during the day. While climbing at 25,000 feet, Joe announced that he was unable to read the instruments, I took my head from the radar visor and found that my eyes were not a lot better, so we very gently returned to Kabrit to be met by the ambulance, they filled us full of salt and tucked Joe up in sick quarters for the rest of the night. However the Meteors were delayed and the Mosquitoes were getting tired: I do not understand the technicalities but there was a tolerance on a glue joint which was measured periodically and aircraft were scrapped if this tolerance was exceeded. The MU however was getting short of replacements so a technical conference decided that the tolerance could be increased to keep us going, but after another month or so there was again a shortage of aircraft, and a further technical conference decided that perhaps this tolerance was not so important after all and could be ignored!'

The end of the Mossies

'However we were not finished with the Mosquito. When our Meteors were delivered the ferry pilots took a Mosquito back with them but left several behind under repair in the MU: these were returned to the UK by squadron crews as they were repaired. The last one, RL141, was appropriated by our CO, Sqdn Ldr Cogill, who chose me to accompany him home where I enjoyed a month's leave – that and the week in December 1952 being the only leave I had during my two-and-a-half year tour. We left Fayid on 24 July 1953, refuelled at Luqa and at Istres, where we spent the night, and arrived at Benson on the 25th. In terms of today's air travel there is nothing to such a trip; I guess a 747 would make it in about five hours non-stop, the passengers would be fed and watered and it would really be little more than a glorified bus ride. For us it was a good experience because we would get some home leave, but we had to work for it. When we landed at Benson we found oil running back along the port engine nacelle and dripping off the tail, so I guess that engine wouldn't have carried us much farther. So a total 10 hours and 45 min. flying time at last had us home. I believe that this was the last time a Mosquito night-fighter was flown by a squadron crew in the RAF, and it is a great pity that none were preserved.'

Final Checks for Landing

Fuel Check tanks

Radiators Open

Brakes Off, check pressures

Wheels Down and locked

Props. 2,850 RPM on final

Flaps Full on final

The original short rear nacelles are still on the prototype.

Later production nacelles were grafted on to the originals.

At time of press, it is proposed that the famous prototype W4050, which has resided for 53 years at Salisbury Hall should be restored to her 1943 appearance when fitted with two-stage Merlin 70 series engines – the last engines she flew with. The aircraft is configured as such internally, including radiators and engine controls etc. The work to date has entailed dismantling the aircraft and moving it into the main hangar. Prior to this, careful rubbing back of parts of the fuselage revealed sections of the upper camouflage scheme she carried later in the war, when fitted with these engines – see page 21. W4050 retained this camouflage scheme until it was repainted all over yellow in 1972 to represent its original appearance in November 1940. The hangar she rested in for so long was the inspiration of Walter Goldsmith, the owner of Salisbury Hall in 1958, whom once he became aware of the association with W4050 and the Hall, campaigned to acquire the prototype and raise funds for a hangar, so she could come 'home'. This was rather timely as the prototype was in danger of being scrapped. She arrived at the Hall in September 1958 on a Queen Mary trailer (central b/w photograph), just as she had left it some 18 years earlier. W4050 was publicly unveiled on 15 May 1959. (all photographs courtesy Bob Glasby)

The prototype as she appeared from 1959 to 1972, before being repainted all yellow at Salisbury Hall. (Bob Glasby)

SURVIVORS 10

Above: Salisbury Hall – birthplace of the Mosquito, as it is today at London Colney in Hertfordshire. The De Havilland Aircraft Heritage Centre, formerly the Mosquito Aircraft Museum, is a volunteer-run aviation museum. The collection is based around the prototype W4050, three other Mosquitoes and other examples of De Havilland aircraft designs. The house itself is not associated with the museum – the museum being in the grounds nearby. (Stephen Skinner)

Left: One aspect of the preserved prototype W4050 that has always intrigued the author, is of the original structure, what remains from what was built at Salisbury Hall? We can discount the fuselage as that was replaced in February 1941 with the fuselage originally intended for W4051 after the accident at Boscombe Down although the fuselage retains the rear access hatch, ventral bay doors, tail cone, fin and rudder from W4050. The nacelles are the original short units – (see left) with the later production extensions fitted over the ends. The exhaust cowlings are of later design and fitted post-war. The wing is the original. W4050's original short span (19 ft 5.5 in) 'No.1' tailplane (as fitted to the PR. 1/B. IV series i variants) was permanently replaced in 1942 with a (20 ft 9 in span) 'No.2' tailplane which is still with the aeroplane today. The 'No.2' tailplane became standard on all production Mosquitoes from the F./NF. II onwards. (With thanks to Ian Thirsk)

WHAT constitutes a surviving Mosquito? When De Havilland designed the aircraft it was not thinking about it being around 71 years later. The materials used were a means to an end to get the aircraft designed and into service as quickly as possible – there was a war to win after all! Wood has poor long-term survivability if not looked after and the Mosquito suffered like any wooden structure if left to the elements. A case in point is B. 35, TA717, XB-TOX, which was recovered from Mexico in 1979. It looked a relatively complete airframe albeit with a broken back, sitting on its undercarriage under a hot Mexican sun, until the recovery team attempted to dismantle it. It fell apart and all they were left with was the metal structures and a 'lorry load of firewood.' Conversely the post-war scrapping of military aircraft yielded little in a wooden Mosquito. After removal of the fuel, engines, instruments, undercarriages and sundry metal parts, the whole airframe was usually burnt. Whereas in a stripped out, abandoned or even crashed conventional metal airframe, it was if left, ripe for recovery and restoration in these more enlightened times. The author feels that what constitutes a survivor is a completely original Mosquito down to a fuselage, of which he believes that, at time of writing, 22 exist. The rest are what could be considered as major parts in store, of which there are around 12, although these figures are a little hard to confirm as some 'airframes' are in private hands and their status is difficult to ascertain.

Some of the complete airframes in the UK and US today are there only by chance due to the making of two movies in the 1960s. *633 Squadron* and, later, *Mosquito Squadron*, gave film stardom to some just-retired CAACU (Civilian Anti-Aircraft Unit) Target Tug Mosquitoes TT. 35s (converted B. 35s) and T. IIIs. This undeniably gave them a reprieve from the scrap man (though three were intentionally destroyed during filming, with another two scrapped after filming was over!) In Canada, a civilian aerial survey company, Spartan Air Services, imported nine B. 35s and one PR. 35 in the 1950s from the UK for aerial mapping. Three out of the current five Canadian survivors are ex Spartan B/PR. 35s.

On the other hand, what often constitutes 'major parts in store' is the metal assemblies: engines, propellers, nacelles, cowlings, undercarriage units, canopies, tyres, instruments and the multitude of metal fastenings, wiring and hydraulic lines that remain after the timber has deteriorated. Glyn Powell, of Mosquito Aircraft Restoration in New Zealand, has undertaken to recreate bomber and fighter-bomber fuselages and flying surfaces using modern glues, but using wartime production methods. His laudable efforts have offered a lifeline to a multitude of metal parts in a new, longer-lasting airframe for static display or to grace the skies once more.

At the time of writing three Mosquitoes are undergoing long-term restoration to fly: one in Canada and two in New Zealand, one of these for a US owner. Ironically the two in NZ are from major parts.

UNITED KINGDOM			KEY: ● Airframe being restored for flight ■ Static airframe ▼ Major parts in store
1.	Prototype W4050		■ **De Havilland Aircraft Heritage Centre**. Salisbury Hall, London Colney. On public display since May 1959, this famous aircraft is undergoing a restoration to return her to her two-stage Merlin 70 appearance as in late 1943. Completion is due by November 2015, the the 75th anniversary of her first flight. See page 21.
2.	FB. VI	TA122	■ **De Havilland Aircraft Heritage Centre**. Salisbury Hall, London Colney. Ex wartime 605 Squadron, the fuselage was donated to the museum in 1978 from the Netherlands. Undergoing static rebuild using a wing recovered from Israel from TR. 33, TW233
3.	NF. II	HJ711	■ **Yorkshire Air Museum**. Virtually complete restoration using sections from four Mosquito airframes, the nose of NF. II, HJ711, the rear fuselage of TT. 35, RS715, the centre section of Mk XVI, PF498 and the outboard wings of T. III, VA878
4.	TT. 35	TA634	■ **De Havilland Aircraft Heritage Centre**. Salisbury Hall, London Colney. Donated to the museum in 1970, the aircraft has undergone a total restoration and is in the colours of a much photographed wartime No. 571 Squadron B. XVI. Ex *Mosquito Squadron* film star
5.	TT. 35	TA639	■ **Royal Air Force Museum**. Cosford. Ex *633 Squadron* film star
6.	TT. 35	TA719	■ **Imperial War Museum**. Duxford. Ex *633 Squadron* film star
7.	TT. 35	TJ118	▼ **De Havilland Aircraft Heritage Centre**. Salisbury Hall, London Colney. Incomplete nose section, with surviving rear fuselage (separate sections). Ex *633 Squadron* film star (sectioned nose for cockpit filming)
8.	TT. 35	TJ138	■ **Royal Air Force Museum**. Hendon *'Milestones of Flight'* exhibition.

Above: Scrapping – Australian style. RAAF PR Mk. 41s await burning in the late 1950s/early 1960s at Tocumwal in New South Wales. These Mosquitoes were sold to RH Grant Trading Company of Melbourne in 1958. After removal of engines, nacelles, tyres, radiators, instruments and fuel drained, the aircraft were burnt – not much to salvage from a Mosquito! There are five two-stage Merlin 69s lying in the foreground – available for approximately £10 to £20 pounds (Australian) each! Most of these Mosquitoes were converted FB Mk. 40s. The Mosquito in the foreground A52-308, was one such machine, originally A52-199. A52-308 served post-war from 1947 in No. 87 (Survey) Squadron (later No. 87 (PR) Squadron): note the squadron badge on the nose. Note also the Meteor (tail at right) and a C.A.C. built Mustang, also scrapped in great numbers by Grant's. Consider the value of these airframes and engines today! (via Les Homer)

Above: A sad end to a fine aircraft. This TT. 35 Mosquito was photographed in 1958 at Hullavington airfield along with many others in the UK. All had been stripped of engines, radiators, nacelles, undercarriages, fuel drained and were awaiting the final ignominy of being burned. Note the broad black and yellow diagonal stripes on the underside, common to target-tug Mosquitoes. (George Baczkowski via the Calgary Mosquito Society)

The third Mosquito at the De Havilland Aircraft Heritage Centre is a wartime FB. VI, TA122. The long restoration of this aircraft is coming to fruition, incorporating the wing of a Mosquito recovered from Israel in 1980. (Bob Glasby)

The most complete Mosquito currently to reside at the De Havilland Aircraft Heritage Centre is B. 35, TA634. This Mosquito was restored at the museum in the colours of a B. XVI of 571 Squadron, 8K-K, see page 65. (Stephen Skinner)

Mosquito T. III, TW117 during her time at the RAF Museum in Hendon, London. This Mosquito was built at Leavesden in 1946 and took part in the last official fly-past of the type in RAF service on 9 May 1963. It later took part in the film '633 Squadron', coded HT-M. It returned to store and was then moved to the RAF Museum, to be one of its first exhibits. In 1991 it was loaned to the Royal Norwegian Air Force Museum and went on display at its new facility in Bodo in 1994 in the colours of 'TD753', a FB. VI of No. 333 RNAF. In this photograph from her Hendon days, is the artist Sir Terence Cuneo (left) and Leonard Cheshire VC, OM, DSO and Two Bars, DFC, the famous Pathfinder pilot. The occasion was a presentation of the painting by Cuneo of Cheshire's Mosquito FB. VI dropping markers on the Gestapo Headquarters in Munich on 24 April 1944. (via Stephen Skinner)

KEY: ● Airframe being restored for flight   ■ Static airframe   ▼ Major parts in store

NORWAY

| 9. | T. III | TW117 | ■ **National Museum of Aviation**. Bodo, Norway. This T. III was part of an exchange between the National Museum of Aviation and the RAF Museum in London. It has been modified and repainted to represent a FB. VI of No. 333 Squadron (Royal Norwegian Air Force) representing 'TD753'. Ex *633 Squadron* film star. |

BELGIUM

| 10. | NF. 30 | RK952, MB-24 | ■ **Royal Army and Military History Museum**. Brussels. This Mosquito was the last of 24 NF. 30s to be delivered for service with the Belgian Air Force in 1951. It wears the colours and markings ND-N, which it wore when accepted for squadron service in September 1953 – it was retired in 1956 and earmarked for preservation. |

CANADA

11.	B. XX	KB336	■ **Canada Aviation and Space Museum**. Rockliffe (wartime Canadian production)
12.	B. 35	RS700, CF-HMS	■ **City of Calgary**. Ex SPARTAN AIR SERVICES. Stored pending restoration to static condition in her original Spartan colours, not on public view
13.	B. 35	TA661, CF-HMR	▼ **Canadian Historical Aircraft Association**. Windsor, Ontario. Ex SPARTAN AIR SERVICES. Remains recovered in 1996, following crash-landing and fire on 10 July 1956. Total reconstruction started using new fuselage from Glyn Powell in NZ. Aircraft will represent 'KB161'
14.	B. 35	VP189, CF-HMQ	■ **Alberta Aviation Museum**. Edmonton Municipal Airport. Ex SPARTAN AIR SERVICES. Restored as a 'FB. VI' in 1995. In colours of HR147, TH-Z of No. 418 Squadron RCAF
15.	B. 35	VR796, CF-HML	● **Victoria International Airport**. Ex SPARTAN AIR SERVICES. Currently owned by Bob Jens and nearing completion to flying status by Victoria Air Maintenance Ltd at Victoria International Airport.

UNITED STATES OF AMERICA

16.	FB. VI	PZ474, NZ2384	▼ **California**. Ex RNZAF. Flown from NZ to California 1953, where it was registered as N9909F, became derelict in 1970. Believed in store Chino
17.	PR. 34A	PF670, N9868F	▼ Note: this aircraft may actually be RF670 (which would make it a FB. VI). Current status unknown – believed parts only
18.	FB. XXVI	KA114	▼● **Fighter Factory**. Suffolk, Virginia. Under restoration to fly by Avspecs, Auckland, New Zealand. Made possible by new build fuselage and wings by Glyn Powell of Auckland, NZ
19.	NF. XIX	MM625	▼ **California**. With Jim Merizan, though owned by the Swedish Air Force Museum
20.	T. III	TV959	■ Owned by The Flying Heritage Collection. As of August 2011, transferred to Avspecs in NZ for possible restoration to flight.
21.	PR. 34A	RG300	▼ Sold by Jim Merizan to Jim Dearborn around the start of 1999, supposedly under restoration. Current status unknown
22.	B. 35	RS709	■ **National Museum of The United States Air Force**. Dayton. Restored to represent a PR. XVI, NS519 of the 653rd Bomb Squadron, 25th Bomb Group, based in England in 1944-45, which conducted weather reconnaissance flights. Ex *633 Squadron/ Mosquito Squadron* film star
23.	B. 35	TA717, XB-TOX	▼ Remains have passed through several hands following recovery from Mexico. Believed currently owned by Jim Dearborn since 1999. Current status unknown
24.	B. 35	TH998	■ **Silver Hill, Maryland**. Donated to US in 1962. Stored dismantled, but complete – pending restoration for the National Air and Space Museum, Washington DC
25.	TT. 35	RS712, N35MK	■ **EAA Museum, Oshkosh**, Wisconsin. Owned by Kermit Weeks and on loan from his '*Fantasy of Flight*' collection. Airworthy but not flown for some time. In colours of a No. 487 Squadron FB. VI, F-EG, as flown by G/C Pickard on the Amiens Prison raid. Ex *633 Squadron/Mosquito Squadron* film star.

AUSTRALIA

26.	FB. VI	HR621	■ ▼ **Camden Museum of Aviation**. Narellan, Sydney. Ex No. 618 Squadron Highball Mosquito, though it is a standard FB. VI, used for squadron training. Owned by Harold Thomas, being restored to static condition using parts from a number of Mosquitoes
27.	PR. XVI	NS631, A52-600	■ **RAAF Museum, Point Cook**, Victoria. Under restoration to static condition. This is the world's only surviving PR. XVI and saw active wartime and post-war service with No. 87 (PR) Squadron RAAF. For photos of the restoration see www.aussiemossie.asn.au from The Mosquito Aircraft Association of Australia
28.	PR. 41	A52-310, A52-319	■ **Australian War Memorial**, Canberra, ACT. Modified from FB. 40, A52-310, during production in 1948. Put straight into store by RAAF – sold in 1953 to a private individual who wished to enter it in the London to New Zealand air race. Forced to withdraw, the aircraft languished for many years in various locations. It was acquired by the Memorial in 1979 at auction. Its restoration was completed in 1997. It is in the colours of No. 87 (PR) Squadron who used the type post-war.

Main photograph: Tony Agar's superb restoration of NF. II, HJ711 can be seen at the Yorkshire Air Museum at Elvington. This is a composite restoration using sections from four Mosquitoes. The cockpit/forward fuselage came from HJ711, which served with 141 and 169 Squadron. It is preserved in the markings 'VI-C' it carried whilst with 169 Squadron. (Andy Dawson)

Left: TT. 35, RS712/N35MK at the EAA Museum at Oshkosh, on loan from the 'Fantasy of Flight' collection. Owned by Kermit Weeks and originally a B. 35, this Mosquito was built by Airspeed and entered service on 13 March 1947. It was converted to a TT. 35 (target tug) in the early 1950s, for which it served in the following decade between periods of storage. It also flew in the film '633 Squadron' coded as HT-F. It was purchased by Kermit Weeks in 1981 from the Strathallan Collection in Scotland and restored to flight, arriving in Florida in 1987. (William 'Bill' Zuk)

Right: TT. 35, RS709, was restored to represent a PR. XVI, NS519 of the 653rd Bomb Squadron, 25th Bomb Group, based in England in 1944-45, which conducted weather reconnaissance flights. (NMUSAF)

Above and below: B. 35, CF-HML, this ex Spartan Mosquito is being returned to flight by Victoria Air Maintenance in Canada. The photograph above was taken earlier in the restoration. Below, a more recent photograph showing trial fitting of the port cowlings. (Kimberly Ingram)

Above: The fully restored main instrument panel in CF-HML. (Kimberly Ingram)

Strictly not within the bounds of this chapter, but the author felt obliged to pay homage to T. III, RR299. Tragically, this aircraft crashed and was destroyed, killing both crew at Barton, Manchester during a display on 27 July 1996. She had a long flying career, being built in 1945 and spending a good deal of her 51 years in the air, delighting all who saw and flew her. RR299 appeared in the 1968 film 'Mosquito Squadron'. The author had the good fortune to see her display over Salisbury Hall in 1990, commemorating the then 50 years of the first flight of the prototype – and who could not forget witnessing her in flight with her precursor, the DH. 88 Comet, 'Grosvenor House' at the Shuttleworth Collection at Old Warden in the early 1990s – a truly unique event. The dramatic view here, reminiscent of wartime low-level ops, shows her at the 'Salon des Avions de Legende' at Lille airfield in France in June 1996. Mosquitoes operated from this airfield during the war. (Ravery Guillaume)

Below left: B. 35, VP189 was built by Airspeed Ltd at Christchurch (UK) in 1947. It was one of the Mosquitoes purchased by Spartan Air Services in 1954. Registered CF-HMQ, it made its last flight with Spartan on 7 October 1963 and was stored until 1967, when it was presented to 418 (City of Edmonton) Squadron of the RCAF Reserve. It was displayed as 'VA114', 'TH-F' of 418 Squadron at Edmonton, but was put back into store following deterioration in 1975 and was then donated to the City of Edmonton. It was restored between 1993-95 as a FB. VI,'TH-Z', 'HR147' of 418 Squadron and put on display at Alberta. (William 'Bill' Zuk)

NEW ZEALAND

KEY: ● Airframe being restored for flight   ■ Static airframe   ▼ Major parts in store

29.	FB. VI	RF597, NZ2383	▼ **RNZAF Museum**. Parts only
30.	FB. VI	TE758, NZ2328	■ **Ferrymead Aeronautical Society**. Fuselage and parts. Restoration underway, using wing from NZ2382. When completed it will represent FB. VI 'HR339'
31.	FB. VI	TE861, NZ2324	▼ Existence unconfirmed, supposedly forward fuselage only
32.	FB. VI	TE863, NZ2355	▼ **RNZAF Museum**. Parts only
33.	FB. VI	TE910, NZ2336	■ **Mapua**. Virtually a complete static Mosquito – bought by John Smith in 1956, stored in a private hangar in Mapua
34.	T. 43	A52-1053, NZ2305	■ **Museum of Transport and Technology**, Western Springs, Auckland. Originally an RAAF, FB. Mk. 40, A52-19, modified to a T. 43, sold to NZ 1946. Airframe undergoing long-term static restoration
35.	T. 43	A52-1054, NZ2308	▼● **Mosquito Aircraft Restoration**, Auckland. Originally an RAAF FB. Mk. 40, A52-20, modified to a T. 43, sold to NZ 1947. Undergoing major rebuild to flying condition using new build fuselage and wings by Glyn Powell. The metal parts of the original A52-1054 are being used in the rebuild. See www.mosquitoaircraftrestoration.com.

SOUTH AFRICA

36.	PR. IX	LR480	■ **South African Museum of Military History**, Saxonwold. This Mosquito saw wartime service in the SAAF with No. 60 Squadron in the Middle East at RAF Foggia, named *'Lovely Lady'*. Donated to the museum in 1946.

(via David Vincent)

Some photographs of A52-600, ex NS631, an RAAF PR. XVI currently under static restoration by the RAAF Museum at Point Cook in Victoria, Australia. A Hatfield-built machine, it was allocated to the RAAF, and joined No. 87 (PR) Squadron at Coomalie Creek on 4 March 1945. It undertook 21 wartime operations. With the disbandment of the squadron in 1946, it was soon allocated to the Survey Flight, later Survey Squadron, and conducted 19 survey flights up to December 1946 as 'SU-A' (at left, the second aircraft). On 16 July 1947 it was allocated to an Air and Ground Radio School and became a static instructional airframe. It passed to another local Air Training Corps Squadron and was then listed for disposal by the RAAF on 25 November 1954. It was then bought by an orchardist in Mildura who intended to use it as a wind machine, mounted on a turntable with its Merlin engines idling, slowly rotating and blowing wind through the fruit trees to avoid frost damage on cold nights – a novel approach! This never took place and A52-600 remained dismantled on the farm (bottom left) for ten years as a cubby house for his children. In 1966 it was purchased by the Warbirds Aviation Museum and moved to Mildura Airport, where it was stored (below) under cover in a hangar. It remained there until purchased by a syndicate in 1983 which graciously donated it to the RAAF Museum in 1987. It was then stored for some years, until arriving at the museum at Point Cook on 31 March 1998, where it is currently being restored to its wartime appearance with 87 (PR) Squadron. For photos of the restoration see **www.aussiemossie.asn.au** from The Mosquito Aircraft Association of Australia.

(via David Vincent)

(via David Vincent)

(RAAF Museum)

(RAAF Museum)

At the other end of the scale, many 'Mosquitoes' remain as a collection of 'bits' – usually some metal parts and tired wooden components. The remains here are held by the Australian Aviation Museum at Bankstown Airport in Sydney. At right is what remains of the centre-section of the wing that sits within the fuselage (the wings outboard of this have been sawn off, just as they have in the fusealge of A52-600, opposite page 122). Note in the photograph at right the fuselage attachment brackets. This section has, in turn, been sawn in half, with the front section turned 90 degrees to the rear section on the pallet it sits on. Note the characteristic DH white painted finish to the internal wing sections.

The remains held by the Australian Aviation Museum appear to have come from several Mosquitoes. The canopy above is likely to have originated with one of the wartime UK-supplied RAAF PR. XVIs, which were also used post-war (although, conceivably, it could also have come from a 618 (Highball) Squadron, B. IV or PR. XVI, the squadron used both types alongside FB. VIs in Australia). The port undercarriage nacelle at left, and lower engine cowling, appear to have come from a FB/PR Mk. 40/41. Other 'bits' on display at the museum are tyres, inboard wing radiator, Merlin engine, cockpit radio, wind-tunnel model, wing-tip and exhaust stubs. (Australian Aviation Museum: www.aamb.com.au)

Ex Spartan B/PR.35 Mosquito, RS400/CF-HMS was built in early 1946 as a B. 35 and then placed into storage. It saw RAF service as a PR. 35 after conversion by De Havilland, the first such airframe to be converted. It was purchased by Spartan in 1954 after retirement from the RAF and gained the serial CF-HMS (above). It was retired in 1960 and brought to Calgary in 1964. It has been dismantled and moved a number of times since and currently resides in store with the City of Calgary pending static restoration to her Spartan Colours (at time of press). (All photographs this page courtesy Trevor McTavish, Calgary Mosquito Society)

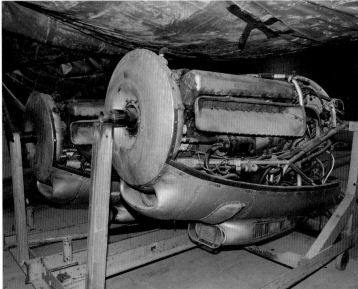

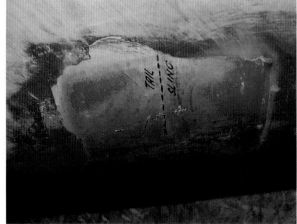

Above: A fascinating relic of CF-HMS's days with the RAF as RS700, remains on the lower fuselage near the tail in the form of a section of the original outer linen and mandapolam covering in RAF PR blue under the later Spartan aluminium paint finish.

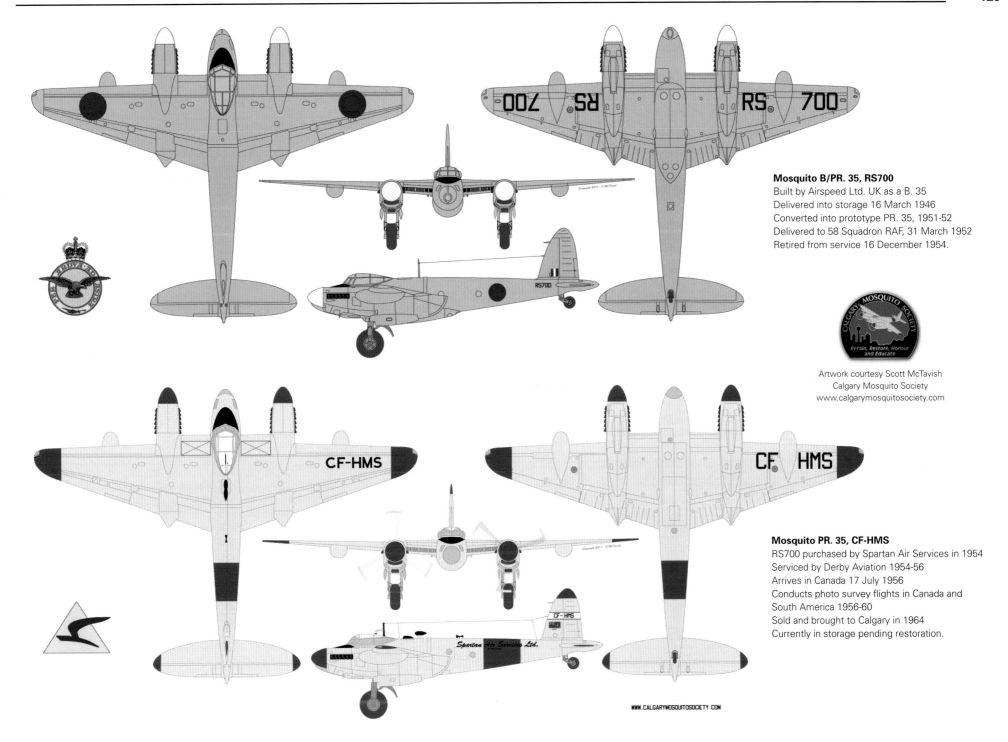

Mosquito B/PR. 35, RS700
Built by Airspeed Ltd. UK as a B. 35
Delivered into storage 16 March 1946
Converted into prototype PR. 35, 1951-52
Delivered to 58 Squadron RAF, 31 March 1952
Retired from service 16 December 1954.

Artwork courtesy Scott McTavish
Calgary Mosquito Society
www.calgarymosquitosociety.com

Mosquito PR. 35, CF-HMS
RS700 purchased by Spartan Air Services in 1954
Serviced by Derby Aviation 1954-56
Arrives in Canada 17 July 1956
Conducts photo survey flights in Canada and
South America 1956-60
Sold and brought to Calgary in 1964
Currently in storage pending restoration.

WWW.CALGARYMOSQUITOSOCIETY.COM

(Allan MacNutt)

Above and below: CF-HMO. (Allan MacNutt)

 SPARTAN AIR SERVICES LIMITED – CANADA

No book on the Mosquito can fail to mention Spartan Air Services Limited, a large user of the type in post-war aerial survey. Spartan was created in August 1946, initially to conduct forestry inventory projects in Canada for the timber industry and later work for the federal government. Spartan used a range of aircraft for its various activities, but growing government contracts dictated the need for an aircraft with increased range and above all, the ability to operate at 35,000 feet with a full fuel load. The Lockheed P-38 Lightning, that could reach this height, was thought to be ideal. Several were bought in the early 1950s and converted for aerial mapping, but operational use presented a downside: the Lockheed was a complicated and high maintenance aircraft to operate, could only fly level at high altitude with an hour or so of fuel, could only carry a crew of two and was expensive to keep flying as time passed.

Spartan began looking for a replacement in 1954, with one of the team arriving in the UK to look at the feasibility of using surplus Mosquito B. 35s which could be purchased for $1500 Cdn each – a bargain. The aircraft was ideal due to its pressure cabin, high altitude rated Merlin 113/114s and greater internal space for the camera equipment. In all, Spartan purchased 10 Mosquitoes (nine B. 35s and one PR. 35). These aircraft were heavily modified for their mapping role with changes to fuel, oxygen, radio, and navigation systems, nose cone and crew comfort. There was also a third crewmember – a camera operator in the rear fuselage to operate the much-improved Wild RC-5 camera (later upgraded to the RC-5a and RC-8). This required major modification to two bulkheads and other internal areas with a modified rear lower starboard access hatch with window and a porthole. Another porthole was later added on the port side to aid natural lighting. Spartan purchased another five Mosquitoes in the UK in July 1955, two of these being reduced to spares at Bournemouth and burnt in 1960 while three were shipped to Canada for spares retrieval. They also operated two Canadian-built T. 29s.

The Mosquitoes ranged far and wide over western and northern Canada in the mapping role from the mid 1950s, including contract work in Colombia, Mexico, Kenya and the Dominican Republic. Five were lost on operations (HMO, M, N, P and R) – three of these sadly with the crews - while one (HMT) never flew operations and was stripped for parts. Another (HMK) was assigned to a subsidiary in Argentina, to become the last Mosquito earning its living in the world. Operations in Canada came to an end in 1962 with contract work drying up and more cost-effective aircraft types becoming available, leaving three Mosquitoes (HML, HMQ and HMS) in Canada. Having done such sterling work, the ageing aircraft were by now becoming expensive to operate and were themselves of little value. Fortunately, out of the three airframes which survive intact in Canada, one is due to fly hopefully in 2011/12 after a long restoration, CF-HML, while another, HMS, is to be restored to static condition in her Spartan colours. Parts from one of those lost, HMR, are being used as the basis of a restoration to static condition.

SPARTAN Mosquitoes

CF-HML, delivered 2/3 May 1955. Last flight 15 June 1963. Currently owned by Bob Jens and being restored to fly in Canada. See page 121.

CF-HMK, delivered 21/23 May 1955. Written off on 22 November 1964 in Argentina as LV-HHN.

CF-HMQ, delivered 9 June 1955. Last flight 7 October 1963. Restored as a 'FB. VI' of 418 Squadron - Alberta Aviation Museum.

CF-HMO, delivered 25/27 June 1955. Fatally crashed near Manitoba, 9 August 1955.

CF-HMM, delivered 17/18 August 1955. Fatal crash-landing, Dominican Republic 27 March 1960. (See Chapter 5, page 66, top photograph).

CF-HMN, delivered 11/14 September 1955. Lost Bogota, Colombia, 22 January 1956.

CF-HMP, delivered 25 October 1955. Fatal crash near Manitoba 10 September 1957.

CF-HMR, delivered 2/4 November 1955. Lost Pelly Lake 10 July 1956.

CF-HMT, delivered 10/12 April 1956. Did not fly - stripped for spares.

CF-HMS, (first PR. 35) delivered 16/17 August 1956. Last flight 1960. Currently in storage in Calgary awaiting restoration to static condition in her Spartan colours. See page 124-125.

CF-HMM in foreground.
(Bomber Command Museum of Canada)

CF-HMK. (Allan MacNutt)

(Allan MacNutt)

DE HAVILLAND DH 103 HORNET – A scaled down Mosquito

Finally, mention must be made of the Mosquito's 'little brother' – the single-seat de Havilland DH 103 Hornet – in many eyes, the pinnacle of piston aircraft development of the 1940s. The Hornet was a most remarkable aircraft due to its handling and performance. The well-known British test-pilot, Captain Eric Brown, placed the Hornet at the top of his list for pilot enjoyment out of the 500 types he had flown. He described it as the 'Grand Prix racing car' of the air, with immense surges of power, 'like a zooming rocket' for manoeuvres in the vertical plane and for aerobatics '... sheer exhilarating joy'.

The DH 103 Hornet was conceived during the war, based on Mosquito lines, but smaller, as a single-seat, long-range fighter. A first for a British aircraft was the use of handed engines (opposite rotating airscrews) to help counter swing on take-off and an overall improvement in general handling. The Merlin engines fitted were known as the 130 series; the 130 was a conventional right rotating airscrew fitted in the port nacelle; the 131 had a left rotating airscrew fitted in the starboard nacelle. The Merlins were also unique in that their frontal area dimensions were dictated by the basic engine block and cylinder head – all engine accessories being relocated, thus leaving a very low profile power unit in a streamlined cowling. The prototype clocked 491 mph!

The Hornet was also unique in that it took the Mosquito's construction methods a stage further – wood to metal bonding, using Redux glue – a first for de Havilland and soon adopted by others. This bonding was used heavily in the wing with the fuselage generally following Mosquito practice – ply-balsa-ply.

Too late to see wartime use, the RAF used four types post-war: the F. Mk.1, PR. Mk.2, F. Mk.3 and F. Mk.4, with a good many in service in the Far East and operating against the Communists in Malaya.

The handed engines made it perfect for carrier use and soon three types were in service with the Fleet Air Arm: F. Mk.20, NF. Mk.21 and the PR. Mk.22.

It is of the greatest shame that no Hornets survive intact today.

'Party Trick' – Hornet F. Mk. 1, PX275, gliding with both engines feathered. This was a routine devised by the Kelly twins – who flew together on the same RAF unit. This involved four consecutive loops, the first using both Merlins. At the top of the second loop, the port Merlin was feathered; at the top of the third loop, the port Merlin was unfeathered and the starboard feathered; at the top of the fourth loop, both were feathered! This Hornet subsequently served with the Central Fighter Establishment at West Raynham, 1946-47, coded GO-F.

A 64 Squadron F. Mk. 3 with extended fin area, photographed in 1949.